bytes BEYOND borders

The Odyssey of a Pakistani Expatpreneur

GHAZANFAR IQBAL

BYTES BEYOND BORDERS: The Odyssey of a Pakistani Expatpreneur

This is a work of creative nonfiction. While the events described in this memoir are fundamentally true, certain details and characters have been altered or fictionalized for the sake of narrative cohesion and to protect the identities of the individuals involved. As such, they are not intended to be read as word-for-word transcripts and unequivocal facts but retold in a way designed to evoke emotion and meaning. In all cases, the author has attempted to honor the essence of dialogue and happenings as accurately as can be presented from memory.

Interior Formatting and Cover Design by: Edge of Water Designs, edgeofwater.com
eBook Design by Iryna Spica, irynaspicabookdesigner.ca

ISBNs:
Paperback: 978-627-94500-2-9
Hardcover: 978-627-94500-1-2
EBook: 978-627-94500-0-5

In homage to Mehfooz and Iqbal—my parents, who not only ushered me into this world but also supported and sculpted me into the individual I have become today!

TABLE OF CONTENTS

PREFACE

Who am I to write a book, especially one about my life? Is my journey, encapsulated in *Bytes Beyond Borders*, so impactful and eventful that it warrants sharing? Or is this merely a mechanism to garner visibility? Perhaps it's a blend of both; certainly, writing a book was never a consideration until several individuals close to me nudged me to do so. Their persistent inquiries eventually led me to acknowledge this idea; thus, I extend my gratitude to them here. After all, what validity does any endeavour have without someone to affirm its worth? Mustafa Hamza, a colleague from one of the unicorn start-ups in which I worked, was the first to breathe life into this idea. He even suggested a few titles. While it may have been on a lighter note, the idea lingered, and it was further cemented by Taha Tahir, a friend from one of my fellowships with an impact organization. After hearing my tales during our weekend chats, he was adamant that I should embark on this writing journey. Coincidentally, I was approached by a book publishing service around the same time; they found me on LinkedIn, and suddenly, it seemed as if the universe was signalling me to proceed. As you take a deep dive into my life story, you'll notice that I tend to follow my instincts, that I leap into the unknown even amidst echoing cautions not to. Each time, fear is present, but the prospect of what lies on the other side is too enticing for me to maintain the status quo — that's simply not my style. *Bytes Beyond Borders* primarily serves to offer something enduring to the world, something that will linger even when I am no longer here. It is a narrative that transcends boundaries, both geographical and metaphorical, providing a connection to this realm and a means to give back to the community through the lessons gleaned from my experiences. If it manages to alter even a single person's life, then this book has fulfilled its purpose.

1

OUTSIDE IN

The northern Arabian Sea is a space to get lost between breaths. Everywhere you look resembles another photo inside a Microsoft Windows background theme with some exotic title like *Saffron by Sunset*: mountains of layered rocks that jag and take bites out of the soft sand; the loneliness of a solid blue horizon; a late-day sun dashing like a fiddler crab into a cave where Portuguese carvings tease a complex history.

Sometimes, like that one time, at Ganz Beach, clusters of small boats—four or five that have seen better days, stacked to near sinking with crates—float just offshore. Lanterns glow in the predawn light and shouts in Balochi, a dialect of Balochistan, ripple the sand. But that time, where usually only waves crashed, AK-47s fired warning shots.

We were friends for the weekend. Adventure seekers. Uzair, a scuba instructor from Karachi, was our leader in every sense—planner, driver, diffuser of awkward moments between strangers. His spirit was daring; his heart was genuine; and his wit was Thal Desert dry. He and I were brothers in misfortune in that we had both been wronged by corruption—him for speaking out about an oil leak that had shut down his ocean adventure business, and me, for keeping my hands in my pockets when regulators sniffing at the door to my start-up asked for a bribe. Uzair had brought Ali, a quiet guy with a passion for loud shirts, and Najid, a former navy sailor, along with a half-dozen men and a few couples whose names I don't remember. We camped, listened to music, and drank forbidden things. We were safe in the shallows until we weren't. Until the smugglers came.

The bigger the wave, the deeper we must dive, as in business.

Most Pakistani parents teach their children to fear the water. *You will drown*, they say. Smart parents scare their children using risk statistics. *People who swim are more likely to die*, they say. Regarding open water, Pakistani parents can't be bothered to monitor or to teach. Such is the way of it when an entire nation gets lost between the breaths of modern society and dirty realism.

When Uzair's four-wheel-drive vehicle bogged down in the wet sand, we camped for the night. We decided we would seek locals in the nearby village to help us dig out in the morning. And so, we had no way to flee, when the strangers swarmed us. Pinned as we were between cliffs on both sides, our backs against the sea, they owned the hills before us, our access point and only possible escape route. Hilux trucks crowded us, their engines idling loudly.

I was the first out of my sleeping tent. Others in our party stumbled awake with messy hair and foul, hangover breath.

The smugglers, dressed like locals in the traditional tunics and long white turbans of the Balochis, studied us like artifacts from a long-ago civilization. A few plunged into the sea to reach for the smuggled crates. One man acted as leader. He had stretched-out features and a neck scarf of a *chum-chum* pink colour that seemed mismatched to his impeccably sculpted beard and permanent frown lines. Maybe he had a wife, a woman who cared enough about him to wrap his neck in a soft, pink cloth. Maybe that care coexisted with mercy.

Daylight lifted the horizon's heavy veil to vibrant honey-orange tones—

an extraordinary backdrop for the snipers stationed atop the cliffs. Their rifles were aimed at us.

The walkie-talkie in the leader's non-gun hand chirped. He responded and then grilled us. His dialect was incomprehensible.

Uzair responded first in Urdu. "We don't know this language."

Chum-Chum butchered his Urdu, but his meaning was clear: *Why are you here?*

"We are camping. We have ladies with us—our families. We heard about this place . . . and it's beautiful. So, we camped."

I had never heard Uzair so repetitive, so flustered. That this friend, a man who had conquered the underwater tunnels of the Blue Hole in Egypt's Red Sea, where nitrogen causes divers to lose their minds, was losing his mind with the smugglers. I felt the urge to throw up, but there was nothing in my stomach.

The smuggler clipped unintelligible words into his handheld radio.

"What . . . what's in the boxes?" Uzair indicated the boats.

No! Uzair, what are you doing?

Ali came to stand beside me at an arm's reach, close enough for me to hear him mutter, "They'll kidnap us. Hold us for ransom. We'll be killed."

Between breaths, I was lost. Death was nothing more than vaporous thought. To speak it, to allow it legs, was to send a body's nerves scuttling sideways into the sea.

"You know," the smuggler said in broken Urdu. "The usual stuff."

Uzair frowned. "What's 'the usual stuff'?"

Shut up, man. We don't care.

"Everyday use. Snacks. Juices."

The smuggler's answer seemed reasonable to my sleep-and-hangover-and-panic-addled brain. I wanted the boxes to be filled with everyday use. Snacks. Juices. I clung to his answer like it was a buoy in a riptide.

"For all these boxes . . ." Uzair crossed his arms. He dug recklessly into a pocket of confidence. "How much could I pay you?"

The smuggler's grip flexed on his weapon. He took a step toward Uzair and sucked salty air through his teeth, teeth that were far less perfect than his beard and hair.

"You cannot afford what's in those boxes."

Arms. Drugs. Certainly not mango juice and Iranian chips.

"No, no. Tell me how much."

"No need." The smuggler stepped away. He had grown tired of the game.

This is not the way to die. I grabbed Uzair's arm. "Man, why are you arguing with them? You'll get us shot."

Uzair had a death wish. All those cave dives. All those times he tempted the ocean to take him. He wanted to die and intended to bring us with him. No other explanation existed.

In my pocket was my identification card that showed I was from the Punjab province. As a kid, I'd heard stories that if you went to Balochistan with a Punjabi address on your card, you'd be executed without hesitation. I thought of my wife, standing on a rooftop in Lahore that Independence Day night, fireworks bursting like pieces of a shattered mirror reflecting the celebration below.

"What were you thinking?" She had shouted to be heard—to *finally* be heard. "You always do this to us. Are you crazy? You have a family now. What were you thinking?"

We were friends for the weekend. Adventure seekers. Nothing more but a whole lot less.

Who am I to write a business book?

Walk the aisles of any bookstore and business books line up like colourful soldiers of fortune. A few select covers face out like the brigadier my father was in the Pakistani army: proud, tempting in their boldface, shouty words, their jackets shiny in all ways but the insides, which matter most. Some say that being the offspring of such a man brought me favour in this life. I argue that favour atop a heap of fossilized dung is still dung.

It doesn't work in the tech space, where I belong.

For me, Pakistan is my crazy first love. With time and distance, most things that made me fall out of favour with my homeland drift away, lost. In that sense, you'll find parts of this book unreliable. I do my best to remember the gemstone-green fields of Multan and to appreciate the labour invested in creating them. I remember inner-city Lahore's narrow lanes and crowded alleys that made life feel urgent, like it had you by the throat and might take you down at any moment. And I remember what it felt like to gaze upon a centuries-old mosque, some of the grandest architecture on the planet, knowing that slivers of my ancestry could be held accountable for such magnificence. These memories, however, do not induce nostalgia. I don't long for the spaces of my past. Rather, the professional I have become is grateful for my land's dysfunction. Pakistan informed the man I am and the legacy I hope to shape.

I came from nothing, felt like nothing, and was nothing—a complete outsider in every sense.

And yet . . .

There are many ways the business world establishes borders. Much of this inside-looking-out perspective is unintentional, but no less harmful. Educational borders exclude those without formal education or prestigious academic credentials. Borders of industry and experience keep out those from other sectors and foster professional scepticism among colleagues. Social borders encircle closed or exclusive networks that limit the free exchange of information among the larger group. Borders around entrepreneurship hinder dreamers' access to investors, capital, resources, and networks of established players.

And then there are the unforgivable borders. Borders of gender, diversity, orientation, age, and culture. The business world pretends it has addressed these borders and that they no longer exist. As a brown person, I assure you that these borders are still in place.

The business world continues to pay the heavy price from erecting these imperfect, manufactured barriers and looking the other direction. We are hypocrites—expressing a desire for a global community but leaning back into a mindset of regional fear and exclusionary practices.

I am an expatriate of borders, you can be too.

My achievements have crossed one of the harshest borders in the world. Politically, Pakistanis are an employment risk. Only three countries—Syria, Iran, and Afghanistan—are statistically less desirable regarding passport power, and most of the Western world cannot say how Pakistanis differ from them. I now work for one of the most formidable global companies, yet I cannot hop on a plane to go where opportunity strikes because I must obtain special permission from embassies; even then, I am sometimes denied entry. Linguistically, I can flow between three languages and seven dialects. English was an essential part of my school curriculum, but my sentences spill out more enthusiastic than perfect. Culturally, I remind people that undesirable and traumatic things have happened inside a history that I had nothing to do with.

And yet . . .

I defy expectations. I am stubborn and pushy. I have been exactly where you are, a business outsider, and I have no intention of leaving you behind.

Stick with me. We'll cross borders together.

Each chapter in this book revisits an essential touchpoint of my Pakistani story. I am nothing without my story. Lessons abound beneath the cultural veil. This book in your hands uses no boldface, no shouty words. Though I cannot speak for all marginalized people, I can speak from their hearts. Inside is what matters most.

Oh, and there is one more border we all share. Perhaps the most troubling border of all.

I felt like nothing. I was nothing.

The biggest border bisects you. Self-doubt has all the hallmarks of the harshest border on earth—barbed wire where you once felt free, terrain that seems to shift and destabilize your footing, a mountain peak whose summit stretches beyond reach, an inflexible gatekeeper who denies you escape from your internal monologue.

Together, we'll cross that border too.

No borders. Just solid blue horizon ahead.

Inside Out in Business

Corporate culture is inherently exclusionary. Unless you're in a senior position or your manager slips up in casual conversation around the water cooler, you don't have access to insider information. In fact, corporations often establish systems to ensure that people who try to access information beyond their pay grade are fired. In these environments, substantial changes that impact a workforce—everything from layoffs and transfers to changes in benefits packages—reach employees as a surprise.

No one likes surprises.

I used to work inside a semi-national company, a fertilizer company, in Pakistan. I landed that coveted job through an odd mixture of hustle and military pedigree. I had the privilege of pushing shit because my father was important. Every quarter, the board of directors met to discuss the distribution of dividends to investors and the bonus allocations for employees. My co-workers and I were on a strict need-to-know basis, but that didn't stop us from incessantly inquiring about our additional compensation. It was Pakistan; we all had loans to pay. But desperate people leak unreliable information. If we heard anything about the finances, we didn't trust the numbers were accurate. Quarterly profit data and growth figures were the mouldy bread handed out to the weakest in the chain of command after the insiders had had their fill. This is the way of corporate culture.

To be fair, there are times when opening information to larger groups of people creates large problems. The eruption of chaos and its ensuing aftermath can be hard to control on the back end. And corporate carries other perks. The budgets? Whew.

Start-up culture, though, is more inclusive. It's hard to hide dysfunction or poor performance in a start-up. Founders tend to divulge more information because they're out in the world talking about their business and seeking investors. Wise founders capitalize on this inclusivity. They emphasize group ownership, either in employee mindset or financially in company stocks, and often share (or cannot hide) their vulnerabilities. That openness leads to trust.

But the inside can be a stressful place. You're taking that roller-coaster ride with your founders and fellow employees, and there are a lot of highs and lows. Their vulnerabilities become yours. Your existence is fragile and fickle. Sometimes it's a be-careful-what-you-wish-for scenario.

As you contemplate your journey from outsider to insider, reflect on the environment that helps you be your best. Do you become anxious when things don't go as planned? Or do you thrive inside the unpredictable? Do you find comfort in knowing that the heavy load of difficult decisions is not on your to-do list?

There is middle ground. Your company's information is out there. You need to know where to find it. A quick internet search will yield the websites and apps that provide a secure space for employees to anonymously share company data, trends, and other insider information. The goal is to level the playing field so all employees can make informed decisions regarding potential employment. Are these reliable sources? Only you can decide. But knowing the type of business environment that best fits your personality and keeping independently informed of what's available, is all better than just accepting where you've landed in life: pushing shit—literally in my case at the fertilizer plant; figuratively in yours.

Beside me on the golden beach, Ali tunnelled his bare toes in the sand and told Uzair, "Let them do their thing, and let's leave."

Najid, the former sailor, approached the smuggler in charge of offloading the boats. "We have women with us. Families."

Again, the repetition of *women* and *families*. A not-so-subtle reminder. As if murder and chivalry might coexist on the same moral compass.

"Our car is stuck," Najid continued. "You have the manpower to push us free of the sand. Otherwise, we must walk to the village and bring more people to this beach. A few pushes now, and we'll go our separate ways with nothing more than stories of an isolated beach and an empty bottle of booze. We all have things best hidden, brother."

The boat captain took in the stares of his comrades and gave a slight nod. "Let us first clear our boxes."

We collapsed our tents and gathered our things while two dozen men in tunics moved crates from boats to the Toyotas. From a distance, Chum-Chum studied us. After digging trenches behind our vehicle's tires, three or four smugglers helped us push free. We shook hands at our vehicle's back bumper and tried not to flee like we had trafficked jellyfish in our trousers.

Again, I became lost between breaths.

Later, locals from the village told us that some border officials give Iranian smugglers advanced warning of when they'd be patrolling in exchange for a cut of the profits. And that we were lucky. Not everyone meets with such a favourable ending.

Balochistan is Pakistan's largest province. It is a site rich with natural gas, abundant resources, and unprecedented diversity. It is hauntingly picturesque, like a Microsoft Windows background. But this globally advantageous region is mired in political and economic instability. Pakistanis cannot get out of our own way. We cannot break our barriers.

And that is why I left.

One of the first things I did when I broke free?

I entered the ocean at sunset. It was pink and glossy and merciful.

You have a family now. What are you thinking?

"Just walk," said my friends. "Take a few steps."

Waves rippled at my feet and stole away the sand. My footing became unsure.

"Go deeper," they said.

Slowly, slowly, I was up to my neck.

The bigger the wave, the deeper we must go.

2

EMBRACE YOUR INNER MIRASI

A genie named Ainak Wala Jin is sent down to Earth by the emperor of genies. Ainak Wala Jin has poor eyesight, which apparently is beyond the scope of genie magic to fix. This is only the start of his misfortune, though. Ainak Wala Jin also happens to land in Pakistan.

I felt his burden on a mitochondrial level. I still do.

But a boy rescues him and takes him to a doctor, who prescribes the thick, dark-rimmed glasses that would have made him a verbal punching bag were he not a magical being.

Lucky bastard.

I'd held off telling anyone for as long as possible. I made it to grade 7 before confessing that I couldn't read anything beyond the reach of my bamboo-stick arms. I was convinced my mom would take away my Sega gaming console. Surely, to her, staring into the pixilated images for hours on end was the genesis of all evil—and near sightedness. At school, my preferred seat was at the back of the classroom, near the wall, because I wanted to be a termite who ate his way through the educational system undetected, a silent destroyer of my own dreams. I self-sabotaged because what others said of me was crippling. *Your life is over. What are you doing? Are you stupid?* From kids my age, those words were digestible pulp—dismissed as crippling insecurity and the pecking order of youth. But from a father, a man who commanded a brigade of military personnel in the Army Medical Corps—those words were an infestation.

"You're running behind. Go, *Chotay Sahab*."

Qadir bahi was one of Father's assigned drivers, one with staying power. He was a Pathan of medium stature with a modest beard and an easy laugh. His Urdu, with a Pashto dialect, sounded rich and confident. His fearlessness in Rawalpindi's chaotic traffic was fabled. He possessed almost nothing but the keys to a car he didn't own.

We'd parked outside the army public school gate in Multan. I thought of diversions to stretch time. We discussed things such as the art of kite flying and the majesty of starry nights in the Cholistan Desert.

"You promised to teach me to drive," I said excitedly.

"I'd as soon drive the Karakorum Highway blindfolded," he said. Karakorum? That was one of the world's highest paved roads, snaking through the mountains all the way to Khunjerab Pass at the Chinese border.

"If I wear my glasses?"

"That would indeed be the eighth wonder of the world." His grin created eye wrinkles too numerous to count. "This is something fathers should teach sons."

"*Abbu* has no time for me."

"He has no time for a son who doesn't try."

Qadir bahi had been saying that for as long as I'd known him. "Besides, you're *Ustaad* Qadir bahi, Genius Driver."

The warm buzz of his laughter nearly vibrated my seat and penetrated my skin. "You surely have learned politics from your *abbu*. Go, before he fires me."

"If I put them on now, will you take me on a driving lesson later?"

Qadir bahi nodded. "Don't tell your father."

I reached into my pants pocket and withdrew the monstrosity. Opening the black arms was like unfolding the legs of a praying mantis that had become entangled with twin magnifying glasses. I was sure Father's white Suzuki Khyber idling beneath us weighed less. I slid the eyeglasses on my face.

"Like a young Shaan."

"Movie stars wear *sun*glasses," I protested.

"If he wore eyeglasses, he'd look like you." Qadir bahi nudged my shoulder. "Try today."

I exited the passenger door. Qadir bahi usually did not let Ghazala, Nasir, or Nadia ride in the front with him. I was his *Chotay Sahab*, his small sir, the co-pilot in his cockpit, Pakistani Air Force—though we both knew they only accepted candidates with perfect vision.

In grade 7, the army public school divided the group of male students. Those who want to try must pass through a rigorous admissions process and, if successful, are sent to a prestigious military academy; those with marks like mine, well, we remained in the standard educational curriculum. I held no illusions about my forward path, but it was the mandatory vision test that outed me.

The Khyber pulled out of sight.

Military police officers humoured me on my trek into the building, inclining their heads respectfully. At the very least, they did not laugh. They knew the consequence of such things. But the children at my school were less seasoned. They were mostly military brats, transferred to any of the four provinces on a whim, hardened to the ways that bonds could bite.

I was Ainak Wala Jin until lunch, when I sat alone in the classroom, listening to shouts beyond the window from the impromptu cricket game—"Boundary!" "Dead ball!"—expand in the heat.

And then I was me.

Personal Branding, or Finding Your Story

In Pakistan, *ajrak* is the craft of block printing on textiles that creates decorative fabrics in traditional patterns. It's an artful use of resist printing. An artisan carves geometric or floral patterns into wooden blocks—usually sycamore or pear wood—then applies a resistance paste to the block before stamping it onto the fabric in a gridded pattern. Natural vegetable and mineral dyes, typically in deep reds and blues, are applied to the fabric. Then the cloth is washed, rinsed, dried in the sun, and the stamping is repeated before the fabric is oiled.

At any step in the process, variants can be introduced: the pressure used to stamp the blocks, the intensity of the colour palette, the amount of resistance paste applied.

Ajrak is a long process. Many craftspeople work alongside nature to move the textile toward a one-of-a-kind finished product. At every stage, the process embraces what is organic.

Entire business books have been penned about personal branding. Having a personal brand is necessary for navigating the current business climate. My intent is not to recycle a business term, reframe it, and dish it out to you in new packaging. Largely, what's been said before is spot-on. But some of it feels disingenuous, as if a three-inch-thick pearwood block is being used to stamp out results.

For those of us who begin with an outsider perspective, our carvings only sometimes seem to fit the desired print. We feel the same resistance, organic variants, and laborious wash-and-rinse process as insiders, yet we do not feel like art.

Personal branding is nothing more than putting yourself out there with thoughtful intent so that people remember you. It is the intersection of all parts of you, but especially where organic meets craft to produce a one-of-a-kind cloth.

I'll show you what I mean.

In 1996, I created a Dreamweaver website for an Islamabad non-profit and earned my first paycheque. This was right after my matriculation papers; for readers not familiar with the term—grade 10. With my five thousand rupees, I purchased a guitar.

My parents didn't like that guitar. For my mom, a deeply religious woman who believes music is not the right path to salvation (because some cleric somewhere made such a statement), the guitar represented a corruption of my soul. My father, a high-ranking military doctor, cared less but still did not like what the guitar implied. To my mom, musicians were *mirasi.* "You don't want to become a *mirasi* man."

My parents' opinions did not stop my younger brother, Nasir, and I from forming a doom-metal band, writing angsty lyrics, and growling vocals into microphones.

Resistance paste, for sure.

I went through an explorer phase. *Mortal Kombat II* and my Sega megadrive weren't enough technology for me. Early internet was slow and expensive, and my appetite for discovering the world beyond Pakistan was insatiable. Exploring involved finding Wi-Fi passcodes to faster servers and becoming someone else. Even with the impending peril of Mother chasing me through the house with her slipper, I ran toward technology.

People who graduated from large universities used to intimidate me. I admired the smoothness of their English. They knew so much about the world and economics, and I was just a dumb kid from a small village in Punjab. Regardless, I sat beside them and listened to them. I allowed them to challenge my mindset and belief system. I still welcome the opportunity to feel insignificant, small, and humble because it balances the moments when I am on a stage, microphone in hand, looking out over thousands of people. A little like a *mirasi.*

I bristle when people say, "You'll never change your passport" or "You'll never get asylum" or "You're not good enough" or "You're out." I'm no longer the kid who hung his head and did the walk of shame away from all the times he tried, *really tried.* I'm no longer the kid who wrapped dance sticks with decorative tape for a rhythmic performance or soared over makeshift hurdles in a gymnastic competition only to be told, "You're not doing it right. Leave." Being an outcast made me who I am today. Now, I welcome people telling me that I'm wrong. I dig deep; I make things right.

A recent search on LinkedIn revealed the following feedback from my peers about me: persistent, good communicator, excels at learning and development, connects with people from diverse backgrounds.

From these snippets, the tapestry of a personal brand takes shape. I'm a *mirasi.* I'm tech hungry. I'm bulletproof. I am the intersection of everything I put out into the world. But where my organic stories meet my skills? I am a cloth not unlike an *ajrak.*

And so are you.

Reasons for Personal Branding

Remember how I define personal branding: putting yourself out there with thoughtful intent so that people remember you. *Thoughtful* and *intent* are the only portions of my definition under your control, so we'll focus on those. Both require higher-level planning than simply keeping up with your social media posts. To inject meaning and land results, you should know *why* personal branding puts you on a fast track to the inside.

Personal branding elevates your visibility over that of your peers. Whereas their online interactions seem random and unfocused, yours are thoughtful. You post about your expertise, values, and the rich textiles of your backstory that shaped you into the professional you are today. In a competitive environment, hiring professionals and others looking at you to fill their opportunities value a focused narrative.

Personal branding also establishes your authority on a subject or subjects. People look to the light. When your brand shines a spotlight on areas where you excel, you build a reputation for those illuminated skills. You will be remembered for the light.

When that focused light attracts others, you are seen as an influencer. Professionals who would benefit from your light begin to see you as a valuable part of their network. Partnerships and collaborations may form.

Like *ajrak* printing, your personal brand is crafted over time, impervious to moods and trends. Individuals who are mindful of their brand convey confidence, loyalty, and resilience. In the tumultuous world of business, forever in a state of flux, these qualities are magnetic.

Before we go deeper into ways to develop your brand, some words of caution.

Your brand should *not* be tied to your work history.

Wait . . . *what?*

If you tie your brand to your corporation or start-up—even the most influential in the world—and you will forever be associated with those entities. Not only are you self-limiting your growth beyond those employers as well as reinforcing a potential inability to break free of those experiences to tackle new ones, but you're also conveying to your outside network that your identity is inexorably joined to those businesses, and this may harness you to established and tired ideas. And if one of those businesses ever takes a PR nosedive, you'll be scrambling to set yourself apart, anyway. So, why not take control of your branding from its conception?

I've used the word *focus* before, so I'll reiterate its significance using a different word: consistency. If one part of your brand is working against the rest, the result grates like a discordant note in an otherwise harmonious strum of the guitar strings. Make sure everything you put out belongs in your song.

Developing Your Personal Brand

Personal branding is never really finished. It begins, and it evolves. It's as animated as the individual to which it is tethered.

Your brand should originate from a locus of positivity. Life is negative enough. The hippocampus and amygdala portions of our brain crave positivity. That doesn't mean you inject anything other than authenticity. It's merely a reminder that there is a positive and a negative strainer through which you must sift every situation.

Keep the idea of impact at the forefront of your brand. Not the self-serving kind of impact, but impact that lifts others. No business journey exists in a vacuum. This book is my tribute to those who influenced the professional I am today; but it is also my way to connect those who inspired me to readers who may find inspiration. A cycle of gratitude. When you lift others, you rise alongside them.

Now that you understand what a personal brand is, it's time for self-reflection. I won't tell you to break out a moleskin journal, pipe brain-frequency music through your earbuds, and sip *chai*. I am most grounded when I'm snaking through the lush green mountains of South Asia astride a 150-horsepower motorcycle. What I will tell you is that the following aspects of personal branding never fail to impress me when I'm networking or seeking candidates for new opportunities. We'll call them the Four A's so you can easily remember them. Find your place, find your moments, and let's do this.

> *Authenticity:* Cut out everything you think you should be, all the noise, and connect with something real. You may have to backtrack. Uncover your genuine values and beliefs. Remember that we were (or are) more authentic in our youth before life dictates how we should present ourselves.

> *Aim:* What do you want? *Really* want? If you possess the necessary courage, what is your ultimate goal? Be clear and specific. At this point, it's okay if you don't understand why you're aiming for the things you want. Clarity happens as you embark on your journey and craft your brand.

> *Authority:* Your expertise. Know it. Be able to articulate it and provide evidence to support your claim. Own it. This is your secret sauce in the business world, so protect it.
>
> *Aesthetic:* You don't have to be the most fashion-forward individual to have a pleasing aesthetic. Beyond cleanliness, self-care, and looking like you've given your appearance more than a passing thought, how does your style reflect other aspects of your brand? What style does your industry dictate? What style can you maintain consistently? If you can't find a style where your authenticity meets your industry, find someone with good style instincts and ask for help developing yours. Once your aesthetic is in place, ensure it is reflected in your branding.

Knowing your brand and conveying your brand are two different skill sets that get to the same truth. Getting in touch with your story is an exercise in looking inward. Telling your story is an outward movement, a craft we'll examine in more depth in the next chapter. Storytelling in Pakistan is next level—horror-stories-by-lantern-light next level.

But before we look outward, I want to explore the one thing you must carve into your pear wood, the pattern that must repeat throughout your brand like a stamped grid, the most critical factor in determining a successful path from the outside in:

Mindset.

I grew accustomed to being the dumbest person in the room.

So, too, should you.

Multan is an oppressive town. It has a desert climate with no rainfall and even fewer ways to escape the heat. Most days in the classroom, flies had more energy than we did. We were drained and impatient. A ceiling fan rearranged the air to little effect. During the hottest months, an evaporative cooler imprisoned between two shabby windowpanes blasted a damp stink into a room crowded with thirty teen boys, lowering the ambient temperature to a slightly more tolerable volcanic atmosphere. For the most part, however, we sat in chair-desks that were stained mustard yellow; we were impounded by white walls sparsely covered in tattered maps and charts; and we dreaded the walk home with fat bookbags. We tried not to live inside dreams that pushed us past our borders.

On the next-to-last day of 8th grade, my math teacher called my name first.

The other boys climbed atop their desks. Their eyes tracked with interest what such an extraordinary event might mean.

Teacher Khan had a small moustache and ears that looked like the doors to a battery-powered rickshaw had been left ajar. His voice on a word—any word—made me feel like I'd dropped puzzle cut-outs I'd never be able to piece back together.

He frowned like he'd gotten a whiff of something rank, mumbled, "Hundred," and placed the graded exam in my hand.

I squinted. Habit, mostly. I still hadn't accepted that I was blind to the things I could not reach. A red-ink *1-0-0* sharpened into view.

It was as if someone ignited a ground spinner and set it loose in the classroom. The other boys' expressions lit up. Random conversations sparked.

"Whoa . . ."

"What did he do to get a hundred?"

"Impossible."

My thoughts exactly.

"Something you wish to say?" Teacher Khan urged.

My gaze drifted to a black-and-white-and-green poster above his desk—a sketch of a handsome soldier sporting a combat helmet, a broom moustache, and a confident twist of his lips. *Pakistan Needs You.* The soldier's index finger pointed at me, accusatory.

Did Khan expect me to explain how such an anomaly was possible? Was he expecting a confession of cheating? A chronicle of how I studied so that others might do the same? I *had* studied, but my previous preparations had never amounted to anything but being last.

"Thank you," I said lamely, as if his instruction had been stellar or his grade was a gift and nothing more.

On the way back to my seat, I was Musa parting the sea. The others made space for me. They touched the paper as if it were a talisman to spread blessings. That day, they picked me for their team. My feet were light on the sprint home. I placed the paper so that my dad saw it at mealtime.

Biology scores came out the next day. Again, the teacher called me to the front. A hush fell over the classroom. The other boys needed to believe in something—that a tempest of heat lightning had struck and the world as they knew it would be forever different—or, at the very least, that change was possible. *I* needed to believe in something.

"Thirty," the teacher said.

My heart was a hard marble that clanked to the bottom of its chamber, back to its place of hope.

A few students stuttered out words on an exhale. They drizzled back to their spaces to watch flies drunken from the heat. The universe righted itself. Dreams outside borders were not sustainable.

When I speak to start-up founders, I feel their struggles on an acute level. They often believe that they dreamed outside their borders and that none of it was sustainable. Like they've done something wrong. They second-guess themselves, rebuke themselves for not signing on with a company, collecting a salary, and making their families predictably happy.

But that marble is everything. Growth comes from that marble. I am them, and they are me.

If you are not failing, you are not trying.

Most people in the workforce—your co-workers and the other applicants are up for the same position that you want—navigate their careers using conventional wisdom. They line up stepping-stones of education and achievement ahead of themselves and forget that alternate paths exist. They make transactional connections on social media, but don't really connect. They define the parameters of their box, but never step out of their comfort zone.

All of this is hiding.

And it's a default mentality.

These ways of moving through business are standard. Safe. Expected. And they work until they don't. Until the company enacts layoffs. Until your team is downsized or your position is reimagined into something undesirable. Until you're faced with the unpalatable choice of relocating or resigning. Until you wake up one morning and realize you've been doing the same tasks for so long that your professional growth has stagnated.

And in the same way that most of the workforce—your co-workers and the other applicants—falls into this mindset, they also lean into the same conventional wisdom to crawl away from adversity. They'll rededicate themselves to networking. Bulk up their stale résumé. Drop a few more unfocused posts on social media. Reach out to obscure social media connections.

The insiders become reactionaries.

Their attempts take on the veneer of desperation. They may jump at the first substandard opportunity because they are unsure what is beyond the safe zone. They circle the drain of insecurity because they are exposed to all the growth that happened while they were comfortable. Opportunity will not present itself on a platter and, yet, the majority act as if it will.

When I say majority, I mean *majority*.

Envision a coffee delivery to your workplace. Ten steaming hot cups, their contents slight variations on the same beverage. Now imagine eight have the word *conventional* handwritten on their cardboard sleeve. Your co-workers grab those. Standard. Safe. Expected. You take one of two that reads *opportunity*. The sleeve is your mindset. You and one other co-worker are now at a new level of competition. Tap your cups together. Cherish that connection. Congratulate each other. You've just elevated yourself above 80 percent of the workforce out there.

How do I stay in the mindset of opportunity? I step into my discomfort. I show up. To events, seminars, networking hours, mastermind meetings, and lunches with people I don't know. I show up regardless of my academics. Regardless of my background, my experience, and my exposure. I show up, regardless of where I am professionally. I meet everyone and anyone. Sometimes I'm the only one standing there when a few others show up, but this presents a unique opportunity for me, one that allows me to connect and introduce those people to someone who might further their journeys.

Why do I do this?

Because I'm working backwards.

Working backwards is a philosophy I adopted while employed at Amazon. Amazon launches an idea or product, works its way backward through the snarls and problems that need to be fixed based on customer feedback, then relaunches the idea or product at an elevated and less-problematic level. Amazon plays the long game and is customer obsessed, so customer feedback is at the heart of its evolution. If customers love you, they won't look at your competition.

Recently, I was put in charge of overseeing a new territory. My initial trip was booked and scheduled—attend meetings, connect with my boss, and visit the office. Conventional mindset would have been to go to my new territory, perform my tasks well, do what is standard and expected, and fly home.

Instead, I worked backwards from an end goal of meeting ten to fifteen connections *beyond* the expected, my own MVP, or minimum viable product. I laid the foundation before the trip by posting on my professional social media network: a photograph at the airport with my destination and the caption: *I'm on my way. I'd love to network. Message me.* I led with thoughtful intent. People know my industry because it's part of my brand. I stepped out enough to say, *Hey, I'm here. If anyone out there wants to work with me, let's connect.* Despite my booked week, I met with six or seven new people in the start-up ecosystem. Before my trip, I knew one person there. I met with him. And then, on the back end, I posted to acknowledge my journey of opportunity, cement those new connections, put gratitude into the world, and support my brand.

Being out there is a critical first step. Adding an outcome—something you want—injects structure. And then, you work backwards.

This opportunity mindset extends to all aspects of career. I selectively interviewed for jobs when I didn't need a job. At the time, I worked for a unicorn (a company valued at over $1 billion) start-up in Pakistan that I never wanted to leave. At that time no other start-up in the nation was as successful. As a result, people often reached out to me with opportunities. My bosses heard about me taking interviews from time to time and grew concerned that I wasn't happy. My answer to them was simple: "I am fully devoted to my role and this company. I just want to see what's out there. To gauge *me*. And I'll know what's at my level if I'm seeking a job. It will help me to expand myself for this company and beyond."

From these interviews, I made network connections. People came to know me. I learned what questions they asked and what was happening in different industries. I grew comfortable with the process. I discovered where I was lacking and where I needed to focus to grow.

Employment offers were not my intended outcome, but they came. I'd extract myself from consideration by saying: *This role doesn't seem like the one I applied for* or *Now isn't the right timing,* or I'd mention the offered salary package. Of course, if you are offered a position and want to go for it, do. Congratulate yourself on your opportunity mindset.

If you work for an amazing company, you see your professional life through rose-coloured glasses. Your confidence is high. Interviews reset that skew and bring you back to a more realistic centeredness about your capabilities and your placement in the industry. One-on-one interviews inform you differently from the way three-to-four-person interview panels do. Experiment with them all.

The mindset of opportunity invites building knowledge. I'm a huge Formula One fan. In my downtime, I stream a series that follows drivers and teams. On the surface, little about auto racing applies to the business world. But inherent to that world is politics, last-minute changes that impact outcomes, competition that can overtake you in a millisecond, and strategizing in real time. No matter what content I engage with—books, poetry, documentaries—I try to find a connection to my experience.

Learn where your industry is going. Go beyond merely considering its ramifications and question ways that new technology will transform your role in that industry. Expose yourself to new ideas, new ways of doing or being in the business world. If you don't stay informed about coming shifts in your industry, you may find yourself an unfortunate consequence of that same movement. Everything you want to learn is out there, waiting for you to expand your borders.

On the heels of a crisis, an opportunity mindset is essential. The world is filled with negativity; you shouldn't be. On a macrolevel, almost as soon as corporate or leadership systems meet with adversity, they accept it and pivot to capitalize on the resultant opportunities. One of Facebook's most fundamental philosophies is the constructive pivot when things don't go right: *We have failed, but these are the data points, these are the insights. How do we move forward?* Political crises become opportunities for businesses to move into a region, be part of the solution, and grow. Financial crises flex policies and force businesses to be resourceful and reinvent themselves. On a microlevel, crises like layoffs and loss of income present opportunities for you to reassess values and where you spend your money. They also incentivize you to expand your skill set.

Everything that happens to you in life, professional and personal, is an opportunity to invite a different mindset. The mindset of opportunity, growth, and positivity isn't easy to attain, but it is a choice. It's easy to shift the responsibility for misfortune onto others instead of accepting our role in it. If life happens and you're blindsided, there's something positive to be mined from the experience. In Chapter 7, "Expect Chaos," we'll discuss strategies to take back your professional life when things get crazy. Trust me when I say there's plenty of crazy in my Pakistani history to draw insights from.

Play the long game. Step into whatever causes you discomfort. Work backwards. Grab that cup of coffee labelled *opportunity.* In the short term, you may experience failure, but failure is necessary to grow. And in that crazy, addictive, life-affirming way, adversity reminds you to feel small and humble, means you're exhaling and moving and trying. If failure becomes routine, though, it might indicate a greater issue, and so look to surround yourself with people who fail from time to time, who challenge the status quo, who challenge their beliefs, and who are open to learning and changing directions. You'll evolve and stretch in ways you never imagined.

You'll work your way from the outside to the inside.

Life is a continuous pilgrimage. Why not invite experiences along the way?

I was rarely picked for anything, but I was chosen for this.

I suspect my dad's status had something to do with it.

Allow the brigadier's son to participate. It will be good for the parents to see, walking into the school. Besides, how can he screw up a welcome?

After all, no one should stay invisible all the time.

Ten 5th graders welcomed families to an after-school event. It was the age of mixed-gender education. We would not be separated by gender until grade 7. We straightened our uniforms—navy trousers and light-blue button-down shirts for boys, jumpers for girls—and stood in two rows, one on either side of the entrance walkway beneath the Shisham trees. Boys clapped. Girls tossed marigolds to symbolize good fortune and to honour the parents' role in their children's education.

"Do not leave your positions," the head teacher instructed us. "You must stay until all parents are welcomed."

Parents streamed by. I clapped as if my applause could raise my dismal marks.

From the direction of the school, my sister Nadia appeared. In all ways, Nadia was a moth. To call her a butterfly was to ignore that she was rarely welcome and most often a pest. At age seven, her eyes loomed large in her slight face, she flitted about in small corners and stairwells trying to find places to land and write and draw, and she obsessed over the colour pink; so, though she had not yet developed Mother's beauty, she was, at the very least, a primrose moth. Nadia clenched her hands and frowned.

I thought she might have to visit the toilet.

I waved her over.

Her lips puckered into a pout. With an about-face, she ran back into the school.

Ten minutes passed. Then twenty. Still, Nadia did not return.

I replayed our exchange in my mind. Had she thought my wave was an indication to get lost? To return to the building? The sun was setting. Far from this event, the second-grade hallways would be growing dim and stifling after being closed for the afternoon.

I searched the faces of my co-cheerleaders, then glanced back at the school's west-wing windows. Enthusiasm drained from my claps. The girl beside me whispered that I wasn't doing it right and made a stink face.

Were all girls moths?

I thought of Nadia, alone in the classroom.

I remembered my time alone in the classroom, listening to shouts beyond the window from an impromptu cricket game—"Boundary!" "Dead ball!"—expand in the heat.

Sometimes, I turned the classroom in that midday hour into a sultan's palace with blue and gold ceiling tiles in a mosaic that mimicked the Arabian Sea and sky. Sometimes, it was a marketplace crowded with vibrant colours and people like me who bought and sold futuristic gadgets, superhero abilities, and all things video game. Sometimes it was an arena of computer circuits where digital guardians engaged in epic battles of heroism or an enchanted version of Punjab with glowing orbs and mythical creatures. Always, there was a bridge. *Roshan-e-Pul.* In Urdu: Bridge of Light. Magnificent in scope and detail, the bridge separated the physical world from the worlds I created.

My bullies could not cross *Roshan-e-Pul.*

Nadia did not have such skies and market bazaars and arenas. She did not know about the Bridge of Light.

My clapping slowed. Again, I glanced at the school.

And then I ran.

The stink-face girl shouted after me, "What are you doing? You're not supposed to leave!"

By the time I reached Nadia's second-grade room, at the farthest reaches of the school grounds, I was drenched with sweat. The late-day sun plunged below the buildings of Multan and turned the horizon a turmeric yellow. The ceiling tiles were a golden mosaic. An Arabian sky if ever I imagined one.

Nadia sat in the middle of it, alone. Her eyes loomed large in her face. She was still a moth.

She was my moth.

I led her by the hand on the long walk back to the entranceway, placed her in line beside me, and encouraged her to clap and toss marigolds.

The head teacher scolded me for disobeying her. I don't remember her words; they were like all the other times I let someone down. Stink-face girl giggled at my misfortune. None of it mattered in the world of superheroes and mythical creatures.

Nadia flitted about.

I laughed.

My parents arrived then. My mom looked like a butterfly. Dad waved and played the part of a sultan prince.

He has no time for a son who doesn't try.

Dad gave me a glancing pat on the shoulder.

It was enough.

3

TELL STORIES

Abde was the storyteller.

He had receding hair, earnest eyes that alighted with talk of all things supernatural, and scars from the stories he refused to tell. He was middle-aged, old enough to have done the forbidden and seen things he shouldn't have, yet his heart was young enough to understand that horror tales told around a campfire were peak summer vacation.

We tried on horror like a coat. Sometimes, in a developing world, it was practice for reality.

Breaks from school meant a drive to the village of Shidani Sharif, a hundred kilometres from the nearest city of Rahimyar Khan. I waited until the last minute to pack for these sojourns, hoping Mom would change her mind about us spending time in such a remote place. Usually, the village had no internet and no electricity past dark. Campfire and kerosene lanterns were more reliable than the province's grid. If the power in Pakistan's cities failed for three hours, rural villages endured for six.

We roasted corn, stargazed, and listened to music until the extended family accepted the fact that our genetic lineage had been stripped of all singing talent and we sounded more like injured animals in the night. The freedom from the distractions of technology and the shared laughter finally made me appreciate the village. The adults would wander away and cluster elsewhere to discuss politics and smoke pipes. That's when Abde would bring out a slate of fresh stories that were hardly fresh at all. Fear recycled well.

"A lone driver was on a midnight journey . . ." Abde would begin.

"To where?" My younger brother, Nasir, was typically the first to interrupt.

I nudged him. "Be quiet. Let him tell it."

Abde went on to describe how, at the driver's previous stop to refuel and grab a bite to eat, he had heard talk of travellers who'd seen by the roadside the figure of a woman in need of help. "These travellers pulled over to assist her, only to go missing and never reach their destination. The driver dismissed the stories as rumours started by locals to discourage people from traveling the dangerous switchback roads at night. He returned to his car and continued down the road. Not three kilometres ahead, his headlamps captured a woman at the roadside, thumbing for a ride."

"What did she look like?" Nadia asked.

Likely, she expected "like a princess" or "a beautiful fairy" as an answer. But as her brothers, we were more than happy to supply her with answers: "like a decomposing half-woman, half-Markhor with bloody, spiralled horns." After enough of these responses, Nadia would frown and be quiet.

"She was dressed in scarlet bridal attire," Abde said, his eyes shining. "She looked nothing at all like in the tales he'd heard. Still, the driver did not stop. He told himself that he had a timetable to keep and someone else would be along soon. But a few kilometres farther ahead, he saw the same woman at the side of the road, gesturing for a lift."

"He should help her. Someone bad could come along."

We grinned. Nadia had not picked up on the impossibility of seeing the same woman in two places while traveling down the highway. She was not yet seasoned to Abde's stories. I placed my hands over her ears.

She wriggled free.

"With an accelerated heartbeat, the driver pressed harder on the gas," Abde continued, "hoping to put distance between them. When he spotted her a third time, his fear multiplied exponentially. Desperate for human companionship, to assure himself he wasn't losing his mind, he searched for another roadside stop, a place for refuge where he might find others so he wouldn't be so scared."

I straightened my eyeglasses. No way I would be stranded in the darkness as the weakest blind one when evil spirits and pranking cousins lurked.

Abde leaned forward. His voice quieted. Beside me, Nadia held her breath.

"The driver glanced in his rear-view mirror. The woman in her crimson wedding dress sat in his backseat. Her blood-red lips stretched into a slow, terrifying smile . . ."

The fire crackled. A gust of wind rustled the trees. Overhead, kikar branches came alive.

The lantern went out.

Likely Nasir.

Nadia gripped my forearm.

Storytelling in Business

Now that you've uncovered the intersection where your authentic self meets your business journey—your personal brand—it's important to become a great storyteller.

People crave stories. Compelling stories engage us, entertain us, and enlighten us. The best stories reveal something about ourselves and about our way of being in the world. Great stories remind us of our humanity.

Sounds like a lot of pressure.

It's not.

Once you're clear on your brand and you remember to lead with authenticity and connect with others from a place that lifts them first and you second, sharing yourself becomes the most natural thing you'll ever put out into the world. You won't hesitate. Why? Because you are confident in your story. You won't be concerned about coming across as a braggart. Why? Because you're thinking twice about your audience and putting yourself in their position. Best of all, the perception of being an outsider changes the more you share. Through your brand, you're inviting others into a shared experience. And the more people who join you, the more you become the insider you wish to be.

Every day, you're meeting people. You're going out and impacting the world. Why can't your brand be part of those interactions? Some perceive this as selling yourself. Maybe. But the hard reality is that if you're not selling yourself, who will? On a fundamental level, if you're not showing who you are and what you can do, you are forgettable. Forgettable people are passed over for opportunities. Forgettable people are overly concerned about being a show-off to the detriment of opening themselves up to be seen. *Really* seen. Forgettable people are replaced.

The goal here is to be remembered, but remembered for the right things. The good things. The things that capture your essence and leave others better than when you first encountered them. Out of sight, out of mind.

I met an Amazon Web Services solutions architect once who said, "Man, you are everywhere. You're super active. I run across your posts and events all the time. I don't know how you do it."

We talked about his social media activities over the previous week. He had shared his travel itinerary, photos he took on the way to a meeting, and a joke exchange with a co-worker that made him laugh. I told him, "You're as active as I am. So why not bring people along for the ride? Share photos of something beautiful you spotted out the window on your rideshare trip. Kind words from a doorman who wished you a productive meeting. Sunrise behind the jet that will take you to your next destination."

"It mustn't take so much time."

Ah, yes. Time. It's estimated that the average person wastes three hours per day on non-productive tasks. How much time does writing a social media caption take? Thirty seconds? Are you optimizing your commute time? While you're waiting for your morning coffee to brew, you have time. Sometimes a more personal aspect of your story takes longer to tell. Occasionally slowing down to produce something more thoughtful is a good thing. But consistency and frequency do more to advance your brand than longer posts with weeks or months in between. You want to be remembered, so remind people. And now, with the advent of artificial intelligence (AI) tech, drafting is even faster.

As an outsider, at first, I struggled with how to bring words together to share my story. I'd rewrite things, worry over what I'd written, and read and reread the words. All of this takes time. Knowing three languages and seven dialects doesn't always mean I use all of them perfectly. So, I trained myself to write less more frequently. Sometimes I use AI technology to rephrase a sentence or two when I'm struggling to eloquently capture what's on my mind. Mostly, I speak from the heart.

Structured content such as in essays and video scripts and on teleprompters have the potential to rob you of authenticity. Speaking from the heart guarantees that you come across as genuine. Storytelling is so much more than spewing words. Even if your words are not the best, even if your vocabulary is wrong, even if you stumble and the only thing you have going for you is your emotion and a connection with the audience, you'll create an impact.

You'll be remembered.

People crave stories. Let's talk about how to tell the best ones.

Determine Your Audience

You will not serve every side dish of your brand to everyone all at once. Though social media posts you create can and should be appropriate across multiple platforms, each site has a unique vibe that aligns nicely with different aspects of your brand.

I run most posts and updates through all mediums. Some social media sites lean into more visual and personal aspects of your brand; some are designed for professional networking. Before you activate your post, ask yourself: *Is this post engaging the right audience here?*

Your goals also determine suitable spaces to share your brand. Is your ambition to work for a specific company? Become an influencer in your lane of expertise? Grow as a person? Start with the fundamental idea that you want to be seen and strategize from there. If you want to be noticed by a specific company, discover what employees of that company are discussing. Filter their ideas through your brand in the online spaces those employees frequent. If you want to become a big deal on a social media site to generate income as an influencer, research the age demographics for that site and adjust your content accordingly. If your goal is personal enlightenment and to elevate yourself as a human, your audience likely won't be found on a career-oriented social media site. Find more flexible areas of the internet that cater to those with open minds and free spirits.

Allow your *why* to be the biggest determinant in finding and growing your ideal audience.

Build Your Campfire

Had Abde told us of the lonely driver and the woman in the red dress in a different place, we might have tuned him out. Stars sparkling overhead evoked another time and place. Flickering flames in the firepit darkened the world outside our circle. The anticipation of the story we knew would come—a thriller, Abde's specialty—connected us and the memories of those nights.

Your campfire is the collective virtual space where you'll gather those you wish to inspire, uplift, and inform. Determine how you are most comfortable creating content. Would you rather write your experiences or hit record on your phone and capture the moment in a video? Is having an archive of your content important? Perhaps so you can write a book someday? Or is it more worthwhile to capture snapshots of now? Which format do you have time to create in so that you are doing it consistently? Which format helps you capture your most authentic self? Vlogs and video-based platforms invite audiences to share a different experience with you than your twice-weekly blog posts or text-plus-photos of your life can give them.

To move from an outsider to an insider, you should have a strong internet presence. But social media is just the beginning. Find speaking and networking engagements, consider a website (especially if blogging is a platform that interests you), be a guest on a podcast, volunteer your expertise with those less fortunate, attend business fairs, and sit on panels to help outsiders with answers to their questions. Find ordinary and extraordinary ways to share your expertise. Invite people to your campfire and lift them. Soon, your network will grow.

You might even need a bigger campfire.

Narrate Your Beginning, Middle, and End

On any given day in business, something is making headlines. Get in touch with what others are discussing. Research topics. It isn't about finding the *right* thing to talk about that will resonate with an audience; it's about opening yourself to all the possibilities of what you could talk about and viewing them through the unique lens of your personal brand.

Recently, Pakistan's government blocked 3G and 4G mobile broadband services across the country because of political unrest. Blocking these services and a few of the major social media platforms deemed to disseminate undesirable content resulted in estimated three to four million dollars in economic losses each day the networks were down. Through my lens of experience and my personal story, I can offer a unique and valuable perspective on how the loss of the internet has a devastating impact on Pakistani citizens and the nation's currency. Speaking about this current event informs those in my audience who may be unaware such an event is happening and also reinforces my brand, which advocates for advancing tech so that Pakistan can compete globally.

Generative AI is another topic with daily developments and far-reaching implications. When I discuss the latest in this area and engage with my audience regarding impacts and strategies to absorb this tech everyone succeeds moving forward. This discussion also gives me openings where I can remind my audience of my skill set and tech background as well, it helps me lean into my mission to lift others.

In these examples, I'm connecting the beginning, middle, or end of current events and noteworthy news to my personal story. I put out content about these topics that comes from my heart. I am passionate about lifting Pakistani citizens so that they can find their creativity, harness their drive, and thus thrive, and all despite a political climate that seems determined to keep them suppressed. I'm passionate about helping people find the right way to adapt to coming technology so that they don't become a layoff statistic. I care deeply about these things, so my audience cares too.

Beyond current events, inspiration is all around. Suppose I am on my way to meet a start-up founder and pass a bicycle leaning artfully against a brick building. What an amazing opportunity to reach back into my personal story and share the moment my dad taught me to ride a bike.

He had presented me with a pastel-yellow bicycle. "Now go practice with the other kids."

I never did. I practiced on routes where I was sure I wouldn't run across the other kids. I wanted to wipe out stunningly in private. Our garden had carpet grass, a dense and padded turf that grew thick. On two occasions, Dad came out to help me, one hand on the steering bar and one on the seat, running beside me. Two occasions were enough for him.

"Do it yourself," he finally said.

I did. That year, I fell more than rain in the Southwest-flow monsoon. But I learned.

Easily, this is a text-plus-photo post. A few inspirational lines about falling and getting back up reach my audience on a universal and emotional level. Who hasn't wiped out spectacularly in a bicycle fall? And who wouldn't like the reminder that no matter the challenge, it can be overcome in the same way as learning to ride?

Or I could use the image to talk about my love of motorcycles and how my ideal method for recalibrating after the workweek all started with a set of two wheels of a different sort.

All of this from someone's bicycle leaning against a building.

Have the Conversation

A conversation is an exchange of thoughts and ideas between two or more people. Your chosen platforms should allow for a two-way conversation. Of equal importance to posting content that aligns with your brand is actively engaging your audience in a dialogue. Ask questions that evoke responses. Take time to circle back, revisit your posts, and respond to comments. Invite responders into your network so that you can further your connection. Respond to their personal brand content.

Listen more than you talk.

The campfires of others are fantastic places for self-growth.

Bring Balance

If I tell stories only about Pakistan or tech spaces, my campfire won't grow. No matter how much interest I generate, no matter my storytelling ability, audiences may find it difficult to relate. As a result, my brand is in jeopardy of being seen as narrow-minded or out of balance.

The 80/20 rule exists for a reason: it works. The rule states that 80 percent of your content should be professional and business-oriented, and 20 percent can be more personal. I suggest further breaking down the 20 percent into 10 percent a mix of personal and professional and 10 percent personal. Although this shaves off more of the personal connection that helps bring people to your campfire, it keeps most of your focus on your professional goals and prevents you from oversharing. This 10 percent pure personal is still crucial to showing a different side of you. Professionals care what type of person you are outside of work.

Remember that 100 percent of your content should align in some way with your brand. Before you share content with any audience, take a moment to ask yourself: *Does this support my personal brand?*

Engender Trust

All is not good about me. All is not bad, either.

I am caught between cultures. I don't always belong. Dad's angry voice still rings in my ears, raising the hackles of self-doubt. Sometimes I have difficulty sorting out what *home* means because my head and my heart cannot agree. I am a tech gypsy with a strong mind and a strong love to give to the world.

When it comes to my brand, I am open. I want people to remember me as a person, not as a facade. Perhaps my candidness reflects my emotional distance from a country that prefers its citizens remain quiet. Perhaps finding my voice after years of living in debilitating shyness is intoxicating. Perhaps openness is a luxury by-product of success. Whatever the reason, I don't have many filters in place.

People trust me.

They should trust you too.

Be consistent. Be authentic. Tell your stories around a campfire built on trust.

We tried on horror like a coat. Sometimes it was practice for reality.

Dad's shouts often came from behind. *Your life is over. You are done because of your marks.* He was a sandstorm blown in from better places. He choked out daylight and made breathing impossible. We tried to protect ourselves, shield each other from airborne threats, and stay indoors, where he felt in control. Sometimes the emotional *haboob* lasted days.

Once, when I was on the phone, he shouted, "Who are you talking to?

Hamad? His father is junior to me in the army, but his kids are doing so much better. Get off and do something with your life!"

Comparing us to military kids in the neighbourhood was as much a pastime to Dad as was taking his nightly stroll, playing bridge on the computer, or discussing the latest news with his buddies. When I was finishing intermediate school—high school in the Western world—with all his money and clout, he couldn't buy me passage into a university. Surprising, given that in Pakistan most things are for sale.

I learned of a technical institute in Multan called Beaconhouse Informatics that issued degrees from an Australian university. Admissions did not look at merit. Expensive tuition excluded all but the most privileged. I studied computer science there. Later, I moved to the school's Lahore campus.

Lahore was the perfect city to escape. Mughal-era architecture was a visual feast compared to the agricultural landscape of Multan. Narrow streets of the old district shouted with festivals and food vendors selling spicy *panipuri* and sweet *falooda*. I frequented gaming cafés on the Y-block of the Defence Housing Authority and immersed myself in multiplayer games like Doom 3 and Medal of Honour. Most importantly, I controlled the prevailing winds.

It was the only thing Dad and I agreed upon—me, gone, was best. Sometimes when you lose yourself in a sandstorm, you end up in a better place.

I wanted to be lost.

I didn't have a place to stay in Lahore and didn't want to ask Dad for money to live. He was already carrying massive university fees, and I had to consider my siblings. They did not deserve a sandstorm at my expense. So, I crashed at friends' places—sometimes apartments, sometimes hovels that barely kept out the city air.

I wandered down to a bus station when I felt like a burden. The Korean company Daewoo had scored a massive deal in the city to upgrade the transportation system. The new buses were sleek blue-and-white capsules with broad windows and seats that reclined. The terminal was open around the clock, and so I often lay on the couches and stayed until morning.

December comes to north-eastern Pakistan like an unwelcome stranger who sits too close and stirs chill bumps on your skin. Fog is common. On a low-visibility night, I arrived at the bus station to find it locked, lights off. A sign on the door read *Closed for Maintenance*. I lay on a nearby bench and watched exhales leave my lips like steam from a hookah until reluctant sleep stole in. I was sure I'd be robbed in the night.

The next day, a friend named Attique picked me up from the terminal. I told him about the falling temperatures, the dampness of my clothes, the worrisome passersby, and the dimensions of a bench better suited to my eighty-year-old *nani*. "Maybe I should change my schedule. Go to classes at night."

"What will that solve?"

"I can crash at friends' places when they're not home."

"You have earned some money now, yeah?"

"A bit here and there. Not enough for rent."

"How much is a bus ticket?"

All the time in the terminal, I'd never paid attention. I didn't see where the conversation was headed. I focused on the mild heat slipping through his silver sedan's air vents and breathed through my mouth to avoid smelling the stale coffee in the cup holder.

My stomach rumbled.

"How much sleep do you need?" Attique asked.

"God willing, more than last night."

"Islamabad is four hours, maybe more."

I did not see how Islamabad solved my problem in Lahore.

He circled back to the terminal to check routes, times, and prices.

"It's perfect," he said. "Each day, get on the last bus to the capital. And then take another bus from Islamabad back to Lahore, fully rested. The buses even have overhead lights to study. Easy."

The plan sounded absurd, but the Islamabad–Lahore run offered the longest sleep for the lowest price. I'd work and attend class during the day and snake my way along Pakistan's highways at night.

"I'll pick you up here each morning on my way to class," he added.

Attique would have absorbed me into his place, but there wasn't room. Already, too many students crowded an efficiency apartment. Given his enthusiasm, he was one cogent argument away from adopting the plan he was proposing for me.

I hedged.

"I'll bring you coffee," Attique said.

I frowned at the cupholder.

"*Fresh* coffee," he added.

The promise of hot caffeine tempted me.

I completed the semester on wheels. Thousands of kilometres, under the vacant stares of strangers, not a *haboob* in sight.

Eventually, Lahore transitioned into the kind of lost I no longer craved to be. I was in the same social circle and environment, talking to the same people repeatedly. Once complacency set in, I realized that I was doing nothing more than wasting time.

I roomed with a series of young men who partied more than they studied. Our apartment became an endless stream of drugs and liquor and girls. Strangers crashed on couches and the trashed-out floor. Guitars appeared, propped against walls. Our band, "Divine Misery," secured a gig at the Al-Hamra Theater in Gulberg. I considered that my parents may have been right about *mirasi* men. Work was hard to come by, and opportunity seemed to have fled.

I craved something to rebalance me, so mornings and afternoons, I visited a mosque. I prayed five times a day. A man who worked for Sui Northern Gas named Asif often prayed beside me. He seemed important and connected, so I tagged along when he invited me to a mosque in Raiwind, where the devout went for sermons and prayers. Asif was, indeed, important, but not in the employment way I'd hoped.

One day, I suggested a new mosque.

"That's a *Shia* mosque."

"Yeah?" A mosque is a mosque, and I had a few months of dedication ahead to make up for my recent debauchery.

Asif looked at me as if I were a *halmasti*—a wolf-like beast that spewed fire—and had suggested a demonic ritual of washing corpses. He wasn't opportunity; he was hateful. Closeted with malice and ill will toward Shi'ites.

Important in the way that he wasn't.

As a child, around a campfire, I tried on horror like a coat. I listened to stories about faraway places and impossible things, never believing they might become reality.

Hate comes to Pakistan like an unwelcome stranger who sits too close and stirs chill bumps on your skin. The fog of prejudice is common. At those low-visibility times, I imagine boarding a bus and watching my home country's highways slink away beneath me. I imagine moving into new circles and clicking on an overhead lamp to remind me that there is still light in the world.

Stories are important.

Your story is important.

Tell it.

4

SEEK OUT THE FORBIDDEN

Independence Day in Pakistan unfolds like in any other country that celebrates its historical fight against colonial rule. Colourful banners and triangular flags snap in the breeze. Children eat too many sweets and foolishly chase the flyovers of military might along the narrow streets. For a day, adults wear *shalwar kameez*, traditional tunics with side splits and elaborate detailing, and pretend the British were the most substantial villains in the land.

That August 14th I stood on a rooftop in Lahore with the love of my life. Saria, my wife, was the one; she had always been the one. She is innocence personified. I call her my *United Nations* because of her passionate efforts to assist everyone around her. She was always the one who calmed my tempests, who understood the short tether between my dreams and ideas, and who perfected words of resilience and strength that rivalled the national anthem: *blessed be the goal of our ambition*. Early on, I knew she was the only one I wanted beyond the *Roshan-e-Pul*, my Bridge of Light—the only one with the power to cross from the physical world into the worlds I created.

That August 14th, of that year, after I'd gone all in on a start-up I lost everything.

Life, disrupted.

Our parents and families did not yet know. From the very inception of the idea, Dad was against it. "What is this *start-up*?" He spat the word like it was a cockroach that had infiltrated his corner of the world and scuttled across his bare foot. "We raised you to work, get a salary, and find a good company. That is all you should want. *Go make babies, get a car, find a home, and live like the rest of us.*"

At the time, my son Ibrahim was 10 years old and my daughter Zaina was 9. Our children did not yet know they'd be pulled from school because we could no longer afford to send them. Saria paced the narrow, L-shaped rooftop terrace where, moments before, the family had dined and then left to join the crowds below, anticipating fireworks. Abandoned chairs sat askew as if blown into place by the prevailing Loo winds. Strings of warm light bulbs crisscrossed overhead and raised a glow rivalled only by the final gasp of a tangerine sunset beyond the cityscape of tall minarets. Yeasty scents of freshly baked naan lifted from the table's empty dishes, churning my already tight stomach.

If a bridge to an adjacent roof had appeared, she would have taken it.

She might have run. Saria was a volcano when her temper flared.

"What were you thinking? This was a huge mistake; I shouldn't have backed you on this Gullu. How will we live?"

I couldn't find words. Music from the revelry below would have stolen my voice anyway.

"You cannot continue to go through life as if you are alone. You have . . . *we* have a family now."

You're failing here and there and there.

Your life is over.

You will drown.

I'd come so far from being the kid in the back of the classroom. I was a *hundred* now, not a *thirty*. I had exceeded expectations. I did not understand her difficulty in remembering where I had been.

"I wanted our lives to be more. More than fertilizer and call centres and this damned place that we'll never escape. Don't I always come through? I always make it right."

"You argue."

"Eventually, it happens. Just the way I say."

"You give logic before you know the right moves. But you're so busy figuring out the logic that you don't listen. I will never be able to compete with whatever it is inside you that pushes you to those edges. Our lives are like this roof—no walls, barely a rail, and a long fall. I don't know anymore. I don't know . . ."

She might have finished her sentence with *what we'll tell our family* or *how we'll survive* or *I don't know if I can do this with you anymore.* I didn't hear her; a sharp zip tore through the night just as the fireworks exploded, creating a canopy of gold and green.

Collective shouts lifted from below. Somewhere, music played. The rich fabric of her expression, the absolute belief in me that had always been reflected there, and what should have been laughter and joy that rivalled the beauty overhead was more like a shattered mirror—glassy, still, broken.

The city had been dry for weeks, but her eyes were a downpour.

Drinking in Punjab is an advanced degree of forbidden. On a fundamental Islamic level, alcohol is *haram.* Because liquor is illicit, you cannot secure it like you can in Karachi, the most populous city in the southernmost province, a more diverse area heavily influenced by a more numerous Hindu population.

In Punjab, to this day, buying alcohol usually goes down like a covert operation: You ask around, someone knows someone, and you call an unidentified number. The person who answers wants the name of the reference who told you. You wait in a sketchy place for a car to pull up. The transaction is made.

In those early days of relative freedom, alcohol wasn't my only *haram*. Trapped by our borders, we explored in other directions—sometimes out of curiosity, sometimes by unintentionally being where things went down. The first time I took the white powder, just after one sniff, I turned into an entirely different person. I talked incessantly for hours. The painfully shy, dumb kid from Multan didn't shut up. Didn't. Shut. Up. In my twenties, this transformation ignited my friends into plying me with other substances to see what other layers had remained hidden.

After a few tastes of the forbidden, in all forms, I wised up. The new Ghaz had nothing to do with the substances swimming through my blood vessels and everything to do with the substances showing me, *me*. Showing me what was possible when I got out of my way. They grabbed hold of the tapes in my head that played the recordings of inadequacy on repeat—*You're failing in physics. You're failing here and there and there. What are you thinking? You'll never amount to anything*—and they broke them.

I learned that I often made forbidden choices to provoke others. To have the opportunity to say, *I believe differently* or *There's nothing wrong with that choice.* My homeland is filled with rules, regulations, and illusions. I have more questions than answers. Why does my forearm tattoo prohibit me from praying because I cannot cleanse the ink from my skin? Why does picking up a guitar and strumming it move my spiritual goal post farther from salvation? Why is being a doctor or serving in the military the only classification of success in Pakistan worth bragging about? From the beginning, I looked outward because I never belonged.

The grandest delusions of all filtered through my mom.

She is the second of two wives. Her view of the world originates in a history rich with a tradition of hiding things from others, especially children, devout attention to all things religious, and the belief that patriotism and religion go hand in hand. "This is our country, and God says this." She enjoys village influence, knows how to play her cards to get what she wants, and prays over my soul that I'll see the light and return to her beloved nation.

A now-dead cleric in Pakistan used to light up our television when we were young. His level of virtue was something she hoped I would aspire to. Tears flowed down her cheeks when she listened to him or spoke of him. "Look at him, Gullu. Look how he talks, how he prays. Why can't you be more like him?" When he died and his underhanded and immoral dealings were revealed, my mom was crushed with disappointment. His character was assassinated, by his own self.

If my mom ever shows up to where I live, my first instinct will be to hide the forbidden. Men in Pakistan are good at hiding more than just their emotions. I don't want my wife and children to see that haunting of the forbidden in me. On occasion, I indulge. It has nothing to do with my spiritual life. They should know its consequences. If I do it more, I sing. Loudly and embarrassingly. If I do it less, I'm prone to deep, philosophical talks. Telling anyone to avoid the forbidden is the surest way to invite experimentation.

Inside what is forbidden, I seek out the *why*. If someone with more knowledge or experience explains why I should avoid something in a way that makes sense, I will make choices to avoid. If I find people's explanations defy logic, I am more likely to lean into the forbidden.

I am the product of a lifetime of rootless restrictions, and so I must work to temper my reflexes and live inside logic and balance.

Had my mom given me a compelling, scripture-based argument about why playing guitar was *not the right thing*, I likely would have strummed it quietly in the corner for a while and ultimately given it up. When she called out the guitar as unseemly, I formed a band and performed onstage.

To Mom, everything outside her narrow lens is objectionable. This includes the internet and the rest of the world that crept in with it. To this day, my parents and siblings remain living inside that lens. My country is still inside that lens. When held up to the brilliant, white-hot, concentrated rays of progress, I worry they will burn.

Disrupting an industry can seem illegal.

One of the first rideshare companies to penetrate Pakistan's borders was an experiment in the unknown. In all the ways that innovation challenges and defies existing laws, progress feels forbidden. Many believed that the company broke rules. The reality is that no regulations had been adopted because ride-hailing didn't yet exist.

Cryptocurrency, blockchain, and decentralized currency feel illegal now. Certainly, those who are not informed tend to cast these disruptions in an illicit light. However, in the future, these innovations may bring stability and safety to economically unstable regions like Pakistan. Right now, Pakistanis experience the sameness and inefficiency of a small economic climate. Life is less than ideal, a certain substandard of living, but it's comfortable, and change is tiresome. Without new, stabilizing forces, the rupee is subject to frequent crashes.

The natural reaction to disruption is to create hindrances—regulations and legal red tape—because these blockades slow the challenge to the status quo. People don't want to accept that industries transition and that their jobs will become obsolete.

I worked in a bank for two months. I left because I could not understand the banking culture. Banks are segmented into two main components: offline banking and digital banking. Digital banking is the future. People working in the brick-and-mortar portion of the bank were forever creating blockades: legal contracts, delayed approvals, procedures about procedures, and meetings about meetings. They understood that their jobs would cease to exist once a bank went completely online.

The same is true of generative AI, which started as nothing more than an algorithm. AI will easily become the most significant disruptor of all industries since the advent of the internet. The future is clear and irrefutable. Artists and creatives are so busy filing legal actions, trying to block or delay it, that they ignore the reality that their jobs will change forever. Adapting or getting out of the way is the only productive mindset going forward.

When we try new things, we disrupt what already exists.

We will also be misunderstood for long periods of time.

All disruptors, at one time or another, are told they are doing something wrong. Curiosity pushes us to question. Questioning is healthy because it reveals negative consequences. At the outset, the concept of nuclear fusion was and *is* promising. Who doesn't want free energy? But how the technology is implemented can create a downside, and make the innovation not worth the risk. In business, the mindset of *something wrong* is often associated with something phenomenal, something great, something impactful.

Humans scare easily. When we try new things, there is so much we don't know. We are programmed to find the pathways of least resistance. We desire a safety net to feel secure. We follow what we're told to do. Society often stops us from taking risks because adhering to well-laid plans benefits the whole over the individual.

And yet, we are inherently dynamic, creative, evolving, and refining creatures. We cannot quiet our innovative, disruptive sides. We all seek more time, more efficiency, more depth, and more understanding.

Finding a middle ground is challenging but rewarding. By leaning into what innovates and what disrupts—the forbidden—I went from hawking products in the smallest towns in Pakistan to working with entrepreneurs at places like Google, Facebook, Apple, and Harvard.

The outside in.

I learned corporate culture working in telecom companies like Jazz, formerly known as Mobilink, and Telenor Pakistan. I had ideas for changes at both. Most supervisors didn't want to hear them. Change is work. Change requires an exhausting string of approvals. Change can be perceived as a threat to job security. Change reveals insecurities. Politics makes change slippery, and most of your co-workers and supervisors have been in their positions for decades. The prevailing mindset of employees is narrow. They've made it. They've crossed some invisible finish line of achievement and can take a breath. Many breaths. Long breaths. Dust has gathered on all they know about what is happening outside the safe walls of their company.

Large and multinational companies dazzle with grand events and fat coffers. The crippling budget decisions start-up founders face don't exist in corporate culture. At the MNCs, we didn't think twice about how many people we could invite, which hotel to book, or the amount of swag to give customers. We conceptualized, exchanged a few emails, and the execution happened, almost as if by magic. Systems were in place. Pampering happened. For the most part, jobs were safe.

Telenor has a substantial global footprint. I travelled to many countries. The company assisted me with visa requirements because I was traveling on its behalf. Travel to Europe is a big deal in Pakistan. The company sent me to Singapore for extraordinary opportunities, including a tour of Facebook Singapore. I earned a good salary. We lived in a nice neighbourhood. Our children attended quality schools. My performance reviews were excellent. On paper, conceptually, I experienced the Pakistani dream. I was at the top. I should not have wanted more. No, not more—*different.* I should not have wanted *different.*

But I did.

I have a bias towards action.

I was in the corporate sector for a decade but wanted something of my own. I wanted to work for myself.

In a matter of months, I'd be standing on that rooftop in Lahore, my life detonating below the exploding sky.

In 2017, Telenor launched a platform called Ignite that invited employees to submit ideas on unique ways our communication services could develop in new digital and service-oriented directions. Winners of the initiative would be given the opportunity to incubate their idea as well as investment money to launch their company or product.

My ideas failed to make the cut.

Twice.

But, the following year, one of my colleagues, Mohsin, who remembered me because of my selection to visit Facebook Singapore, invited me to join him in preparing his idea. He was a strategy and systems specialist. His idea was to connect mechanics with drivers who needed roadside assistance using a mobile and web-based platform—like food delivery to your location, but the service would dispatch technicians. In developed nations, this may sound upside down. But, in Pakistan, consumer demand for used cars is so strong that citizens who can afford new vehicles purchase them as an investment to sell for later profit. Used cars require more maintenance, so why not flip the service model, and bring the repair to the breakdown?

Mohsin was passionate about this idea. He feared he would be out enjoying a motorcycle ride with his daughter and his bike would break down in a dangerous area. He called his idea AutoSahulat. He was a project-management guy, and I loved social networking and sales. When I saw his pitch deck, I was confident it would make the Ignite cut.

My mind tripped ahead. Working on his idea was a step up into a global network. I could escape my daily grind and open myself to new experiences. In hindsight, my enthusiasm had less to do with the idea and more to do with what being involved with Ignite could bring me professionally. I figured Mohsin had enough passion for the both of us.

With AutoSahulat, we were selected into Ignite and embarked on Telenor's three-month incubation program. Mohsin and I received training and mentorship from field experts in Thailand, Singapore, and Norway and refined our customer journey and prototype to address key problem areas. Then, we returned to our original roles at Telenor.

After all I experienced with Ignite, Telenor felt small and confined. One of the vice presidents from the global team told me about the two-month start-up boot camp hosted by Antler, a global venture capital firm based in Singapore. I applied and got in, then asked Mohsin to join me. Our final pitch raised a six-figure, pre-seed investment, making us the first Pakistani start-up to close funding from Antler.

Mohsin and I bid goodbye to Telenor and became entrepreneurs. I finally had my *different*.

Although we were a Pakistan-based start-up, we registered AutoSahulat in Singapore, a requirement of Antler. At the time, Pakistani law required foreign companies to register with the Securities and Exchange Commission of Pakistan (SECP) and obtain security clearance through the Ministry of Interior (MOI). We followed the procedures for both, opened an office in Lahore, hired a five-person team, built our app with the help of a local tech-development company, and started registering mechanics with our platform.

Within a few months of launch, we collaborated with local vendors, won a few competitions, and made pitches to venture capitalists and angel investors at one of the most prestigious tech forums in the world—Google headquarters in Singapore. I was also selected for an entrepreneurship program at Harvard.

It felt surreal. AutoSahulat was live in two cities—Lahore and Islamabad—and scaling rapidly. We were already discussing the next round of seed funding and expansion with investors all over Southeast Asia.

That's when the unknown number popped up on my phone late one afternoon.

Fear

Name yours. Then do it anyway.

Frankly, if you must first think about conquering what you fear, you'll never overcome that fear. Instead, your fear will build and expand. Your brain is already stopping you from experimenting, from experiencing something new, so don't give it the luxury or the time.

If you fear heights, go skydiving.

If you fear water, scuba dive.

If you fear international travel, buy that ticket.

If you fear talking to people, go to a networking event.

To grow, you must feel discomfort. Fear and I are acquainted because I'm still evolving.

On my first day with Amazon, I got nauseated. Being at Amazon felt like I had boarded a rocket ship. G-forces of expectation left me disoriented. I retreated to the restroom, splashed cold water on my face, and regretted everything I had and had not yet eaten that day.

You're failing here and there and there.

Your life is over.

You will drown.

Then I called Saria.

I remembered Lahore. The rooftop. The fireworks. "I am going to fail here. I thought I could do it, but I can't."

Saria is forever the one. She calms my tempests, understands my dreams, and perfects words from her place beside me. There is us, the bridge, and then the rest of the world.

"I don't know anymore. I don't know . . ." I said.

I might have finished that sentence with *how I'll withstand the I-told-you-so's from my family* or *what you'll think of me after I completely disrupt our lives for this* or *if I can do this anymore,* but my voice abandoned me.

"You always say the same thing. Things just work out for you."

"No. *No-no-no.* Amazon is *big*. It's entirely different."

She reminded me of my pattern. Different environments, different countries. The first month, I step into the discomfort and the chokehold of fear. Then I set one-month personal goals on how to perform, connect, name what scares me, and do it anyway. By months two and three, things have fallen into place.

"You do this, Gullu. You set priorities, learn the new system, and then inject the things you love into it."

Someone entered the restroom. Music that played through invisible speakers crept into my awareness. I noticed my reflection.

Somewhere along the line, in the disruption of our lives, that feeling of no walls, barely a rail, and a long fall became accepted. Expected. Manageable.

My own personal Mars shot.

Rocket scientists work under a constant veil of uncertainty. They're undertaking a goal that has never been done before. Imagine the fear. They haven't yet been to Mars. Regardless of the data, they cannot predict the outcome with any certainty. But these scientists engage each day to find creative solutions. They take risks. They step out of their comfort zone and put their next breaths on the line.

The start-up culture is not nearly so life-and-death, but it's no less dramatic to those who engage in the risk.

I sat in the computer lab at Beaconhouse Informatics engrossed in a lecture. It was the early days of college, and I was taking my first steps out of my perpetual cycle of failure. I studied more effectively. I filled in the closest slot to the lectern so that I was not distracted by mint-green walls and photos of the graduate classes before mine.

Outside, Multan felt like a sunspot—bright with intense heat and blinding with the sameness of every day. Inside, the instructor killed the lights. The air cooled, a projector illuminated lecture slides on the white board. After late nights hanging out with friends, the slight hum of the projector's fan was my greatest nemesis.

Again, I can't say why I turned around in my seat that day. Hadn't I purposely sat up front so as not to be distracted? Blinds were drawn. Spaces behind me were dimmed blue and grey in the glowing monitor screens, the way the sky turns in July when rare thunderstorms roll in and excitement builds. I had not heard the clacking of a keyboard or an errant cough. I can't say why I turned around in my seat that day except for the feeling that I should.

Directly behind me, I saw her.

She had a petite frame and a small face. Her eyeglass lenses reflected the lecture's glow. Her straight hair was down and caught the light like poured coffee. Her skin was the perfect shade of creamy brown. She didn't move, likely didn't notice me looking, but a clap of thunder jolted beneath my ribs. I stared for too long, irresistibly drawn, as if a thread of awareness had already woven itself between us and turning away might sever the strand. The lecture slid away. I no longer cared about millimetres and mint-green walls.

The guy adjacent shifted his attention to me. I quickly turned back to the front of the room. I spent the remainder of the lecture gathering the thread, rolling it on itself until I could tuck it neatly away. I learned nothing about computers that day but everything about how a life story changes in an instant. One moment, you're inside the blinding sameness; the next, the sky turns and excitement builds.

That woman was Saria. And I knew that day she would play a significant role in my life.

Start-up Fear and Risk

Few areas in business are as uncertain as the start-up ecosystem.

New challenges happen daily. Two months down the road, you may not know how you'll pay salaries. You're launching a product that's barely been tested. You're hiring unknowns and basing your company's success on them. Investors advise you to reorganize.

Start-ups are chaotic and frugal.

People who have worked in a bank for ten or fifteen years or who come from corporate culture don't always have the experience or skill set to engage in the risk environment of a start-up.

Limitations of Risk

In a conversation about risk, it sounds strange to talk about the things I won't do.

On a professional level, I am open to risks. I cannot see the future, but

I have faith, a positive mindset that frames adversity into opportunity, and I have enough cycles of uncertainty behind me to know I'll land on my feet. There is no stopping what I want to accomplish.

I cannot always say the same about personal choices. On a basic level, I would never intentionally hurt someone. If something doesn't make sense in the long term, I won't risk it. And if it doesn't place Saria and my children first, I won't do it.

If you are family-first, if you financially support your spouse, parents, or children, secure them first. Raise the funding. Pressure will take a mental toll if the money isn't there. If founders come to me with only minimal requirements of income per month to support a family, I will not fund their start-up because I know they are destined to fail. Ninety to 95 percent of start-ups fail, so questioning what is happening in the founders' personal lives is valid.

Over the years, through my experiences and countless failures, my family has come to accept that these journeys are part of me. We've had our downs, but the ups happen too. There is trust and honesty and acceptance that I will emerge as a better version of myself. They witnessed me opening a vein and bleeding into AutoSahulat to make it successful and have come to understand hard truths about why it failed.

Engaging in a start-up is never mandatory, and yet it is part of our global business culture—a trend. Marketing follows trends, so the increase in start-up funding has been phenomenal. Everyone talks about start-ups. Everyone wants to engage in a start-up, regardless of whether the idea is solid.

Today, people ask me why I am not leading a start-up. Second-time founders are more successful. With my experience—through good lightning strikes and bad scary ones—the risk is considerably less than the first time. But risk still exists. I have criteria. To be honest, AutoSahulat was Mohsin's passion, not mine. Automotive repair never excited me in the way that some of the latest advances in technology do. I don't want to copy what works in developed nations and paste it into Pakistan. I have a bias towards action, but I want to innovate. So many start-ups fail because they fail to disrupt an industry. The majority of the time, a copy-paste mentality undercuts a start-up's success.

Only now can I frame in a positive light what happened when that unknown number popped up on my phone. Mindset really is everything. I would be within my rights to have become bitter, but not so long after we left Pakistan, the currency crashed. Politics turned volatile. As if to underscore all that happened in the rapid decline of AutoSahulat, as if my start-up failure prophesized the greater misfortune to befall the Pakistani people, we got out. I cannot say the same about most other Pakistani professionals.

That afternoon, the person on the other end of the line identified himself as an agent of the local intelligence bureau. He wanted to meet AutoSahulat's cofounders to understand more about the company and its funding.

"It's part of the verification process for a company registered outside of Pakistan," he explained.

We invited him to our office. He insisted that meeting at a restaurant was best.

I was out of town then, so Mohsin went to the restaurant alone. The agent brought several people with him. He questioned Mohsin about the business model. From the conversation, it was clear to Mohsin that the agent knew little about how things work in a start-up. Moshin paid for the food. The agent mentioned he wanted to meet me, too.

A few weeks later, the agent showed up at my house. I patiently and politely answered his questions, though I knew his file already contained the necessary information. He probed deeply into my professional background—the companies I had worked for, in what capacity, how long; about Antler and how this start-up was funded. He also asked about my personal life—my parents, where they lived, what they did for a living.

Despite the questioning, Mohsin and I weren't overly concerned. We were upstanding, tax paying citizens with no red flags and a reputable standing in Pakistani business circles.

The business moved forward. But our revenue was not where it should have been. In truth, how many cars break down at any given time? And even if they do, we were reaching only a fraction of them because we were operating in only a part of Pakistan. We realized we were simply getting a commission from the transaction with third-party mechanics, and a small commission at that. We lacked the growth numbers needed to scale, so I wanted to start on the used car market. Mohsin believed that strategy lacked focus. *Let's keep opening the cities*, he said. I agreed because AutoSahulat was his idea, his dream, his passion. I was just the chief marketing officer.

The following month, we received official letters from the regulatory entities that AutoSahulat could no longer operate in Pakistan because we had failed to obtain the necessary clearances. When pressed, their reasons were vague and unclear. Nothing made sense.

Operations were to be halted, effective immediately. After a while, with no resolution of the issue in sight, we gave our team one month's notice and ultimately let them go. I contacted friends in the local entrepreneurial ecosystem to see if anyone had experience with this or could guide us in how to formally protest the ruling. I made a connection within one of the institutions involved, but the ruling was firm. We lost everything because we were unwilling to pay the ultimate cost of doing business in a developing nation.

The agent expected a bribe.

We had done everything right. Lawfully. Mohsin and I refused to taint that ethical history.

We weren't the only start-up this happened to. During the 2020 start-up boom in Pakistan, to prevent what happened to us from happening to them, several start-ups hired retired government officials to deal with the regulatory side of things. If you have a retired official on your payroll, he has the influence to push past the governmental barriers.

All my dumb-Multan-kid life, I had foolishly chased military might along the narrow streets and pretended the British were the most substantial villains in the land.

All disruptors, at one time or another, are told they are doing something wrong.

That hot rooftop evening in August delivered a different kind of independence. I pulled Saria into an embrace, reset myself, learned that I needed a new system, and injected myself into the things I loved: my family, and my appetite for innovation. I had to be there, on that rooftop, so I could be here, now.

When we try new things, we disrupt what already exists.

We're also misunderstood for long periods of time.

5

CRY IN THE CAR

A colleague once proudly told me that FFC, the acronym for the Fauji Fertilizer Company, actually stood for *family, friends, and colleagues.*

Four years before I embarked on my start-up journey to form AutoSahulat, I had been a top-performing junior sales executive at Fauji Fertilizer Company one day and out the next. So much for family, friends, or colleagues.

The first thing I did was come up with an entirely different acronym. *F* no longer stood for *Fauji* or *Fertilizer.* That year was a perfect storm of events that culminated inside a friend's dented, grey economy car.

The second thing I did was to forget myself. I forgot the bro code. I forgot to grip tight to my ingrained Pakistani masculinity. I balled up my dismissal letter with its elite typeface header and logo. Tears, snot, screams, and curses.... so much for masculine stoicism

Not my proudest moment.

"Please help me get this job." I might have clasped my hands in my plea to my friend Talha. "Please help me get into FFC. I don't know if there are any positions, but talk to your dad and get me in."

To make ends meet, Saria took a job in the school our children attended, getting a price break on tuition in exchange. We lived with our parents. They all supported me while I tried to figure out my life and pretend, I wasn't a failure.

"You have to pass a test," Talha said.

"I'll do it. Anything."

FFC was huge. The wizard behind the burqa in the Oz that was Pakistan. Scoring a position meant the restoration of stability and self-respect.

"Buy the guidebook and study," he said. "It has the exam questions and answers. If you pass it, I will try to talk to my father. Before that, I cannot."

For the first time in my life, I studied properly. The way my teachers and parents hoped I would—reading, journaling, memorizing, and quizzing myself on the way to and from places. I took the exam and waited.

At dawn, a few days later, I lay tangled in the bed, watching Saria get ready for her workday. Her beauty stole my breath. With each new copper ray slanting through the window, with each new accessory she put on to present herself to the world, I thought, *It should be me. I promised to take care of her. Now look at what she must do.* I checked my messages.

I had cleared the exam.

I bolted out of bed and lifted Saria into a spinning hug. She fussed; she was running late. I didn't care.

Talha came through and helped me get an interview. The interview was at FFC's head office in Rawalpindi, an eight-hour bus ride away. By the time I reached the building, I was strung out from a day of travel. My shirt, once immaculate, was sweaty and wrinkled. My stomach announced itself in the reception area like it, too, had a scheduled interview. I had not eaten since home. Around me, waiting, were young men who chatted and one-upped each other with credentials: National University of Sciences and Technology, Lahore University of Management Sciences, Institute of Business Administration, and other foreign universities.

I had none of their credentials. I was, after all, a dumb kid from Multan.

The interview panel included retired military personnel, corporate employees, and Talha's father. He knew only that I usually won at poker with his son and landed in many places. I hoped Talha had told him something positive about me to compensate for the gaping void on the application documents. Interviewers sat apart from me at a long glass table. I held down a chair on a carpeted island and formally introduced myself.

A corporate guy in a silver suit rattled off a speech about the process and the position, probably his twentieth speech of the day. Beneath the table, his knee bounced impatiently. He blinked as if he'd just removed an IV of triple-shot espresso but did not make eye contact.

"Why should we hire you?" It wasn't an open-ended question. It was a shots-fired question.

"Pardon?"

The eldest military man's gaze shifted to the late hour on the noisy wall clock.

Clack-clup. Clack-clup.

I had already lost them. All of them.

Suit Guy's response was terse with an edge of impatience. "I mean, look at your academic background. How well could you possibly perform?"

He was Dad all over again.

What are you doing? Your life was over before you stepped off that bus.

I thought of the candidates in the reception area—their blue threads, shiny knock-off watches, and beachy colognes, as if they'd forgotten they were fifteen hundred kilometres from the closest sea. I had none of their credentials, but they held none of my truths.

"You're absolutely right. My past is nothing to brag about. It was a phase. It's done and dusted, and I can do nothing to change it. The other applicants out there in the waiting room *are* academically stronger. Most of them will use your company as a stepping-stone because it's a good brand with a good reputation. They'll work for you for a few months, maybe a year, and the first opportunity they get with Coke or Unilever or some other multinational company, they'll take what they've learned from you and apply it elsewhere. You'll be left to start this process again with another candidate. But I will deliver more. More drive. More strength to overcome. More appreciation for the opportunity. More of everything that they will cast aside in a short period of time. Unlike them, I will stay."

My stomach rumbled its support.

I was strung out. I answered a few more questions and hoped they mistook my frustration for passion. The interview transitioned to more comfortable spaces. We talked about guitars and bosses I'd had before. I mentioned that Steve Jobs and Bill Gates were college dropouts.

"I'm getting there," I added.

Suit Guy gave away nothing, but a few others chuckled.

In the end, they offered me a contractor job because I lacked the necessary academics. For three years, I proved to them everything I said in my interview. I overcame and appreciated and gave them more of me than I ever knew was inside. I brought the kind of substantive change that large corporations allow—measured and slow but meaningful. My professional reviews were exemplary.

Most important of all, I stayed.

Talha's father retired. Personnel changed. Another managing director came, and my contract was not renewed.

The dismissal letter with the elite typeface header and logo was left on my desk.

Pakistani men are indestructible alphas who lack emotion and deliver whatever is expected.

At least, that's what Pakistani boys who grow into those men are conditioned to think.

Muhammad Iqbal, my father, was a decorated military doctor who served in two wars. Nothing that happened in his eldest son's life, no amount of bullying or whining or crying, would ever surpass what he'd seen and heard and done. How can a ten-year-old compete with a father who is a self-made warrior-saviour?

Fight back, he'd say.

Fighting is your way, not mine.

Pakistani men talk about successes, politics, women, and money—not necessarily in that order. Personal problems and feelings are never up for discussion.

Certainly, crying in your buddy's car is unheard of.

Jealousy is also a substantial part of male culture in Pakistan. For every hundred men, there is one job opening. Pakistan is now the world's sixth most populous country at 241 million people. Despite China's and India's populations being five times that of Pakistan, they have figured out how to offer their citizens ample opportunities while we still struggle. Numbers and survival are the game. In some respects, these terrible odds are a barrier to any desirable, long-term outcome. In a much bigger respect, jealousy should be an indicator of the need for honest self-assessment and a shift in mindset. *What have I done? What has he done that might open opportunities for me?*

Not long ago, I started following an accomplished Pakistani man named Saad Hamid on social media. He works at one of the world's tech giants. At least looking from the outside in, he was living my dream. The tired mindset of my homeland, the tired mindset of an outsider, is to look at such an accomplished individual and succumb to jealousy. We tell ourselves the person has achieved so much because of family connections, birthright, educational privilege, or sectarian advantages—the politics of a developing nation. We default to conspiracy theories rather than face the reality that no one gets to a place like Google without taking responsibility for his path.

There is a more productive mindset.

I asked myself, *What has he done?* I thought, *Maybe I can find something in his experience that can help me.* He was connected with the start-up ecosystem. People listened to him. He had an excellent network and had received many opportunities. It would have been easy to lean into the gut reflex of jealousy. Instead, I approached his history with curiosity and wondered how his journey might inform mine.

On his profile, he listed an Acumen fellowship. Acumen was foreign to me. I researched everything I could find about the organization. The fellowship is a program that develops leaders with an entrepreneurial mindset. During my search, I realized I was in the next cohort's application window. I leaned into my brand, told my story, and was selected for the selection process. That same accomplished Pakistani man took part in my final interview. I conveyed to him that I was there because of him, that we were both in the start-up ecosystem, and that if Acumen had been good for him, I believed it would be good for me too.

When Mohsin and I started AutoSahulat, entrepreneurs talked only of successes and scaling. No one discussed failures. In Pakistan, failure is never a positive thing. Not in business. Not in families. Children are brought up to believe that merely passing is not success. Success comes from accomplishing the extraordinary. Being A-plus level. Failures, then, become secrets. No one wants to be the guy who says, "I'm shutting down my start-up because I couldn't make it work."

Contrary to my upbringing, I spoke about my AutoSahulat failures.

I'd say I didn't have the academics others had, but that was okay. Sometimes we cannot have such things in life because of what we have gone through. Such limitations do not mean life ends. Focusing on the disadvantages we carry with us sends us into a black hole of darkness and negativity. Endings hurt, but new beginnings heal. A mindset that focuses on our advantages and how we can bring more wins into our journey is the best route forward after adversity.

Corporate-sector people loved it when I shared my start-up experience—not out of any sense of camaraderie or relief that such a secretive state of being had finally been dragged out into the light, but because I'd left them behind. I'd left companies like theirs and boarded a rocket to grow like crazy. I got global exposure, got funding, and met with industry giants they had only ever dreamed of. I was an outsider who had glimpsed the inside. I left the corporate sector because I thought I knew better. And look where that got me.

They were delighted that I'd been put back in my place, that the universe had righted itself.

After Mohsin and I lost AutoSahulat, after the rooftop, I descended into dark spaces. I questioned my judgment about everything. Maybe I shouldn't have quit Telenor. As Dad reminded me, I'd had everything a Pakistani man should have wanted with that job. I had been at the top and had then crashed spectacularly. Maybe I'd dreamed beyond what was possible for a dumb kid from Multan. Maybe I would always be a thirty and not a hundred.

Conversations with strangers, with people who didn't know me or my situation, those discussions were bearable. The ones with family were more difficult. *This start-up stuff is not for you. You failed at one. What makes you think you won't fail at the next? We told you so? Who calls mechanics to them through a mobile app? It's absurd. You get to know mechanics over time and build a relationship. And, realistically, how many times does a car break down?*

These people were not with me in Thailand or Singapore or Norway. They didn't know what is discussed in a design-thinking workshop. Start-up culture is as foreign to them as a glacier is in Jacobabbad.

I stopped arguing. If they talked, I listened and then left the room. The problem with relocating? Their voices followed and played like a recorded message in my brain. Complete mental torture. Starting again took more effort than I had left in me.

You're a man. Just fight through it.

My brain shut down. Suicidal thoughts poured in.

No one wants to hear what's going on in your mind. This is personal, and personal is never up for discussion.

At that time, mental health services in Pakistan were almost non-existent. Suicide was a criminal offense. Allow that to sink in for a moment. Traumatized, broken souls who come to the most significant crossroads they may ever face and survive face massive fines and a jail sentence. Talk about a twisted pursuit of success in A-plus fashion.

For the longest time—too long—I talked only to myself. In the dark corners of my bruised ego, I believed that others were against me. I tried talking to a few people in my network, but nothing shifted. My mind projected a series of events that could happen: if I reach out to person A, he will do B, C, and D, so why bother? Eventually, I spoke to enough people that I found the right people. People who had been through similar experiences. I moved past the indifference and discovered that others care and genuinely want to help. Kindness is human nature's default. My only regret with the journey back to sound mental health is that I didn't open up sooner.

The route back wasn't easy. Socializing and networking helped, but asking for a job was embarrassing. You're seen as a founder who once raised major funding but now needs employment. A few weeks back, you came to these people to sell them your product, and now you cannot make ends meet. Still, I did it. I never shied away from it. My motivation was Saria, and my kids. I wanted to prove to them that I could make it again. I wanted to prove that those scores of a hundred in my life weren't a mistake. That a dumb kid from Multan could overcome adversity and find success.

My start-up closed because I didn't get the proper documentation from the MOI—an indirect failure with complex circumstances, to be sure. But I had to own the loss directly. I started those conversations with, "I should have known about such things in a legal way. But it happened, and I'm seeking a job because I have a family to care for. You've seen me. You know my skills. I'd be grateful if you'd connect me to the right people . . ."

Taha, a friend I met through the Acumen fellowship, is a social entrepreneur who runs an organization that aims to remove the stigma of mental health issues. He was instrumental in the recent passage of legislation in Pakistan that decriminalized suicide. I was happy to provide a video testimonial for his organization.

People are constantly fed success stories. It's a reinforcing narrative that pushes businesses into a positive light, but it's not always accurate. Few talk openly about the pain on the way to success. I am strong *because* I reached out to others. I am resilient *because* I pushed through my fragility. I am at Amazon *because* I failed.

The *Sohan Halwa* of Business

I crawled out of my extreme shyness around tenth grade. By then, I had built confidence as a video game and computer guy. I looked for kids whose fathers had received recent military postings in our town and who shared the same interests. Our nerdy troupe bonded over Sega consoles and HTML and stuffed down our emotions as if they didn't exist. But resilience, or 'stickiness' comes from the intersection of things we enjoy and the things that challenge us. Adversity versus fun. Which gets you further?

Sohan halwa is a delicacy in Pakistan. It's a nutty, sweet confection made from boiling water, sugar, milk, and flour together, adding pistachios or almonds along with spices like saffron and cardamom, and pouring the mixture into a pan oiled with clarified butter for easy removal. It's Pakistan's version of the West's marshmallow cereal-bar treats and just as sticky.

Multan is famous for its *sohan halwa*. The local shops typically sell it in disc-like rounds. Each batch is a little different depending on the ingredients, but they come together memorably.

Emotions are the *sohan halwa* of business—not necessary to a steady diet of success, but a treat that, when indulged in, brings the stickiness that bonds ideas, people, and customers.

Your personal brand comes alive with storytelling that reaches people's emotional touchpoints. When the universality of experience is made apparent, people are motivated to engage, listen, help, and act. But what if emotions can play a more important role in business?

Emotional intelligence is our ability to effectively manage and regulate our emotions and respond to the emotions of others. For too long, *business* and *emotion* have been mutually exclusive concepts.

It's time for that to change.

Shortly after my start-up failed, I worked for Careem, a regional ride-hailing app that has since evolved into a super-app that delivers groceries and food, manages payments, and connects users with everything from bike rentals to housecleaning. Though my first role was as a sales manager, I transitioned quickly into the position of Country Head Sales to foster corporate alliances.

Careem embraced emotional intelligence.

Each month, team leaders and employees held mandatory one-on-one chats to plug into the company's culture. Back then, I smoked. My colleagues and I would head to the terrace for a cigarette or go out for food or coffee. I steered the conversation away from work. If that person didn't open up first, I did. I'd tell them about a fight with my wife or how my daughter thinks I tell lame jokes and wants to be dropped off so her friends can't see me. I bumped up against my problems in conversation in a way that Pakistani men are taught *not* to do. Almost always, this led to openness on the other person's part. Once those walls are down, the emotional bond becomes unshakable. Even if an employee messes up, he'll come to you. That *sohan halwa* stays with you for a long time.

As a mentor, I had people come to me to say in confidence that they were considering applying elsewhere. After encouraging them to speak with their manager, I'd sit with them and talk about where they were applying and what attracted them to that culture. I'd go through their résumé and suggest changes, and we'd scroll through their social media to ensure that they were representing themselves with authenticity and integrity. I'd remind them to put me as a reference. These were quality people. I didn't want them to leave, but I understood the desire to move on to new challenges.

All of us have a responsibility to make a difference in the lives of others, to make their journeys easier, and to have an impact in the world. Even if all you ever do is connect with others on an emotional level, it's a gift. Business moves on regardless of its people. Things happen beyond our control. There will always be more profits, more expansion, more mergers, and more deadlines. Fulfillment is found in being remembered—remembered for the right things. Good things. Things that capture your essence and leave others better than when you first encountered them.

The Special Case for Empathy

Innovation stems from empathy.

Understanding what people want from their workplace helps leaders create a flexible, stable, and nurturing culture. Home and work may be two different realms, and some employees may seem masterful at keeping their worlds distinct, but the health of one impacts the health of the other. If an innovative policy or structural change at work can better support an employee's family, that loyalty will cycle back into company devotion and an enhanced sense of purpose.

Not so long ago, layoffs cut our workforce in half. Initial instincts are to worry about yourself—*I just took on a mortgage, I just moved here, my wife and I just had a baby, will I be next?* Instead, I remembered my friend's battered, grey economy car. I remembered the snot, the screams, and the curses. I remembered crying in the car.

My throat squeezed shut.

I emailed everyone else whose job was spared. We gathered those who were laid off and treated them to dinner. They are humans first and employees second. I knew they would not reach out to those of us who remained because they were in a different state of mind. They may have considered themselves failures or mistakenly attributed the layoff to poor performance. We helped them where we could, connected them to job leads and networks, and sent recommendations that might help them land on their feet.

When the time is right, when they're past their grief and the crying in the car stops, they will remember. Even if they don't, peace comes to those who are empathetic.

In the battered grey car that day my friend Junaid had displayed tremendous empathy.

"Everything will be fine." He patted me on the shoulder. "This happened for a reason. We'll find you something. I know some people."

"I did everything by the book. I *outperformed*, man. Why does this keep happening to me?"

We drove the city. We smoked a joint. He secured a few interviews for me in the days that followed. And I remember.

That year was a perfect storm of events.

At FFC, I often visited agricultural land for sales calls. My region of responsibility was hot. Temperatures averaged around 49 degrees Celsius; that's 120 degrees Fahrenheit. Our company car had poor air-conditioning. Nearly every customer call was in a small shop awash in fertilizer fumes and no electricity.

I awoke one morning after a gruelling day of sales calls and used the restroom. My right arm dropped like an anchor. I couldn't feel it or control it. I sat on the edge of the bed right about the time the rest of my body failed. Left arm. Then mouth. Then my entire self.

Saria breezed through the room on her way to the closet. "You'd best get your breakfast. You'll be late."

I couldn't speak. My body had slithered down on the bed. I could only stare at the ceiling.

Total paralysis.

Saria backed up and smiled. "Get serious. You'll be late."

I joke around. A lot. It took her a half minute to realize I wasn't playing.

She screamed for Dad.

Trapped inside my body, my mind raced. *It's too early for me to go. I have a family. I have Saria and my kids. I have to provide for them. They're too young to lose me.* The room compressed around a pinprick of light, then went dark.

At the hospital, I regained consciousness. Doctors ran tests. They theorized that something was wrong with my spinal cord. They didn't know. Sometimes when I sleep at a bad angle, I experience the same episode all over again.

My heart equates paralysis with death. If I am unable to be me, I am dead.

Life is chaotic and ever changing. I often thought about the future without realizing the present. After this event, I promised myself I would remember to live for the moment. I got the tattoo on my forearm—three triangles related to Odin, father of Thor—to represent life, death, and rebirth. Waking up in that hospital after the first paralysis was my rebirth. I still plan, but now I remember that I am alive and can do so much.

I cry in the car, in the company of a good friend. I eat *sohan halwa* because it is a delicacy. I share coffee and listen as co-workers become storytellers, narrating their journey. I avoid dark spaces. I talk about my failures because they usher in new beginnings.

And I still joke around. A lot.

But not about that.

6

BALANCE TRADITION AND INNOVATION

Happy Homes Bakery benefited greatly from its proximity to the military hub of Multan. It also benefited from its proximity to my dad. His obsession wasn't so much a sweet tooth, though it might be argued that privilege opened us up to things of excess. The sweet perfume of pastries made him happy in a way few of us could. I often tagged along to remind myself that beneath his hard, crusty layer sprinkled with sugar—not unlike the fried dough balls in rosewater syrup of *gulab jamun*—lay his goodness.

No one exits a bakery in a foul mood.

In the days of his most profound disappointment in me, those days of the *Roshan-e-Pul*, my Bridge of Light, and the eyeglasses that rarely saw anything but the inside of my pocket, those days when I boarded a mental train to faraway lands for long stretches, the bakery was a waystation that pulled me back: walls that peeled yellow like the end of a butter stick cut into slices, glass display cases cool to the touch, the *ding-ting* of the smashed bell above the door, and the occasional hum of mixers in the back room.

The bakery had seen better days, but days had never seen a better bakery.

Golden crusts, elegant icing, and vanilla custard straight from a feast in Jannah. Happy Homes was crowded with goods, always busy, and the one place Father could not ruin.

At least, that's what I thought.

His expectations were eggs we were expected to juggle. Be perfect. Never too loud. Fun is overrated. Finish his sentences as if we could read minds. Clean his plate. Achieve in everything. Never mention the wrongs of adults. Fetch things once he is seated. These were eggs of tradition. Any crack in the shell of his rules did not sit well with a man whose entire identity was tied to enforcing order for the benefit of the republic. Privilege provided us with many opportunities. However, with that excess came a loss of the simple peace we knew in childhood.

Shoes were of particular importance to Dad. They must shine, be laced, be positioned facing out as if we might need to escape in the night and the extra millisecond to turn them around would be the difference between life and death. For all I knew, it was probably true. National security matters tended to ooze down into the families of high-ranking officials. But what upended him most was when dirty shoe soles touched things they should not touch.

His obsession became my obsession—the one egg I refused to drop, for Father's voice rivalled an air raid siren in strength and carried just as far.

I finished placing my order. The bakery was crowded, so I wandered outside while he completed the purchase. My sandals landed in a sweet that had fallen to the dirt. Immediately, I thought of the carpet in Dad's red Corolla and how upset he'd be when my dirty soles touched things they should not touch. I slipped them off and waited on a bench outside in the rising morning heat.

My mental train edged past. I boarded in the way I always did.

Abbu emerged from the bakery like he'd been fired from an assault weapon. He groused about the crowds, the rising cost of bread, and the lack of air circulating in such a confined space. Apparently, some do exit a bakery in a foul mood. He motioned for me to hurry along and get in the car. We made it all the way home before the egg dropped and smashed.

"Where are your shoes?"

I looked down. I didn't remember the sights out the window on the drive back. My train had yet to return.

"You don't have any shoes on your feet."

I remembered the fallen sweet, the bench.

"I put them down at the bakery. I must have forgotten them."

He went from inquisition to air raid in three seconds. Our garage became a one-sided battlefield where I was riddled with shame bullets. *Are you stupid? Dumbest kid I've ever known.* He paced to the car two or three times to search the floorboards. All the while, more bullets came. *They're not in the car. What's wrong with you? You're such a failure. I swear, you're done. Why can't you understand things? Now I have to drive back there. So, help me, boy, if they're not there and I have to buy more . . .*

I don't have a good memory. I forget things. If there is drama, I deal with it, then pack it to be hauled away at the next waystation, never to be seen again. The sandals were right where I'd left them beside the bench. The drive was no more than five minutes. But this core childhood memory is where I began to compartmentalize Dad—and, to some degree, life—for self-preservation.

The many scoldings I deserved from him—like when I took the Corolla without permission and crashed in a ditch—became trunks filled with dysfunction that were best not rifled through. He was a doctor, yes. He was intelligent enough to know the impact of such things on a child. But he was foremost a military man who loaded his family with crates of eggs. Expectations too numerous to juggle.

A product of his background.

Muhammad Iqbal came from a rural village pre-1947, when the British partitioned off the western segment of India so that Muslims and Hindus could each realize political clout. His father, my grandfather, died when my father was in grade 7. His eldest brother managed the household, their five sisters, and a broken and grieving mother. Iqbal joined the army to find better opportunities, became a decorated soldier and doctor, and married twice—arranged the first time for convenience and children, arranged the second time for children and connections.

In the Muslim faith, men can have four wives. They must do justice to them all. It has been stated in scripture, but it's impossible to do in modern times. My wife would kill me.

I heard that my father fell in love with someone during his years at university in medical training. But his eldest brother, whom he considered a father figure, insisted he marry in the family. Father planned to flee to the United States with the woman he wanted to marry. He passed tests, gathered his papers, and planned their exit. His brother found the papers and ripped them to pieces in front of him.

"This is your country, Iqbal," his brother scolded. "Whatever you do in life, you'll do it here. You don't leave."

Father's first wife, my stepmother, had a son and a daughter. Both died shortly after birth. They were named Ghazala and Ghazanfar, like my sister and me. His first wife could not bear more children, so his family pushed for a second marriage within the family—a cousin, Mother. Together, they had five children. To Dad's first wife, he gave his second son, my brother Mustansar. I did not see my stepmother often. She led a close-knit life and preferred to remain in the village where she'd been raised until Mustansar was ready for higher education.

My mom is street smart. She enjoys city life, where she remains connected and influential. Of my parents, I am more closely tethered to her, mainly because of age, though she was the more likely to chase me through the house and pop me with her slipper. The chasm of relatability between

Dad and me is vast—nearly uncrossable. He is forty years older. He prays but is not very religious. We rarely spoke when I was younger because he was busy. I disappointed him, so he eventually distanced himself.

He did not *really* mind me playing the guitar. I liked that about him.

At a young age, maybe that day at Happy Homes, I realized that no one—not parents, siblings, relatives, or friends—would help me, and that was because they'd given up on me. If there were to be successes and trains that took me to faraway waystations, I had to do it myself. My inner voice whispered, sometimes screamed, but when isolation set in, it was my companion. The voice was youthful and strong and often overpowered what society said, so that by the time I reached degree level, adulthood, and professional life, I was already an outsider who had honed my instincts and was secure in dismissing what others suggested.

There are traditions, and there are innovations. They are neither good nor bad but inform the journey ahead. Father had his eggs; I have mine. Everyone has them. This chapter is full of mine—what experience has taught me about the right balance between tradition and innovation in business. It's okay if we drop a few eggs or leave sandals at the door of a bakery. That is how we learn to listen to what's inside and board the train to other waystations.

Modern Business Myths

After the global pandemic, which was a disruption of epic proportions, we as humans innovated. We ramped up remote communication techniques. We reinvented systems to accomplish things beyond our limitations. The collective business mindset shifted. We questioned why we needed to go to the office when we had the tools and technology to work from home.

Everything about that question is spot-on. We *can* work from home. We *do* have the tools and technology. But just because innovation happens doesn't mean tradition has lost its value.

The office environment is a creative and dynamic place. At the office, the two spheres of employees' lives aren't clobbering each other for attention. Rather than emailing, snacking, waiting for someone to respond, or sneaking in a nap (don't lie, we all do it), the same question emailed to a colleague could be resolved faster and more efficiently, with the potential for greater discussion, problem-solving, or bonding, in a shared office environment.

Symbiosis is gone.

The pandemic taught us that there is much more to life than work. A worthy lesson, to be sure. But we've been fed a steady diet of the work-balance myth for years. Work–life balance is an impressive headline that sells books and baits clicks. It makes us feel good and validates the lazy bone we all have inside. At home, we are more lethargic and not at our peak performance. We stare at the inside of our familiar walls instead of experimenting with moving around inside our businesses and networking.

To achieve goals, sacrifices must be made. If you are not sacrificing, someone else will, and you'll be left in their rear-view mirror. Competition aside, it's common sense. Supervisors and managers seek employees who make their lives easier, lessen burdens, and have a team-oriented mindset. If you're the person who never comes to the office and logs off at precisely five o'clock, regardless of which fires are burning around you, no one will care that you desire a work–life balance so you can spend time with family. That supervisor or manager will find someone with a less agenda-driven view of the two worlds. And you can bet that others will put out that fire you so righteously walked away from and left burning. Resentment in the business environment is toxic.

The same holds true for another innovation in the work environment that gets buzzy headlines: the four-day workweek. In theory, short workweeks sound fantastic, as if caring about employees is a top priority. But that loss of productivity impacts the business. When businesses are affected, layoffs happen. Companies are intrinsically immoral. They seek profits. If profits don't happen with the people there, they'll find new people who will turn profits.

Don't fall into the trap of thinking your company is in a love affair with you. That mindset benefits the company, not you. There's an existential crisis to it all. The company will always think about itself over you. Companies are notorious for layoffs ahead of quarterly earnings calls to give their stock numbers a bounce.

The last ten to twelve years have been huge for big tech, and this has meant job security for employees. Growth during the pandemic was necessary and breathtakingly fast but ultimately unsustainable. The industry must balance and reset.

While this happens, look at the reality of your situation. If your work climate changes, you must change with it. Who doesn't want to work from home, achieve work–life balance, and show up for four-day workweeks? Just know that those theories sound great in the media but lack a real-world perspective and that sticking to those theories may ultimately cost you.

The Inertia of Tradition

The version of success we were taught as children in Pakistan is not unique. I suspect similar expectations are implanted across most developing nations. We are told there is only a handful of worthwhile professional paths to pursue: military, medical, and engineering. Why? Because in previous decades, these professions provided security, which is key for people in developing countries. Likely only one person in the household earns a living. Pakistani men usually don't want their wives working, a tradition that cuts out 50 percent of the potential workforce. For Pakistan to grow and compete globally, women must become an integral and respected part of the workforce.

To this deeply ingrained cultural tradition add geographical and political challenges. By not opening up the borders to satisfy the need for diversity, Pakistan's workforce has almost no influx of people from different nationalities and backgrounds. As a result, the same tired mindset repeats, generation after generation; in Pakistan, you are born, educated, work, marry someone from a strong background, make a family, get a better house, and die. You have your roots, so you stay and deliver.

But with the younger generations, this mindset is shifting. Young people don't accept the level of patriotism that holds them back. The internet has given them a global mindset, so borders are less visible. They question sectarian beliefs because they are exposed to perspectives from beyond the echo chamber. But there is still religion, and there are still the political and bureaucratic angles. To question either is ill-advised. People are dying for these beliefs, and economy is collapsing, so it's clear that Pakistan has a long way to go before it will embrace innovation and compete globally.

If you come from outside, if you think like an outsider, you will remain an outsider.

Advanced Innovation

At Careem, the ride-hailing app, everyone had ownership. Team members had assigned tasks but were free to start an initiative if they believed the idea stretched the company in innovative ways. Rogue innovators determined why their idea was necessary, why the timing was right, and what their desired outcome was. If they convinced their teammates that the idea had merit, they were encouraged to take charge of their vision and to go out into the world to get started.

Even if the idea didn't make much sense and never materialized into anything, we looked at this freedom of failure as an opportunity to learn about our customers and products and test our industry theories.

Companies that look beyond accepted rules and limitations win market longevity.

Now my little sliver of Amazon feels like a start-up. It would be easy for a trillion-dollar company to lean into a corporate mindset, but instead this climate is designed to give employees a sense of ownership that enables us to try new things. It makes sense because I am part of Amazon's start-up team for entrepreneurs. To be successful and understand my customers, I must *be* them. Each networking event is a series of details I carry out, end to end, to ensure a desired outcome. I wear many hats in a way that is similar to a start-up founder. I bring creativity and hustle to my role that wouldn't happen under a corporate mindset.

Salary structures ensure that innovation cycles continue. New hires receive a signing bonus that is divided into monthly stipends for a set period, typically two years. After the bonus is depleted, regular pay resumes. Apart from the stocks received, essentially your salary goes down. This is when some people choose to move on from Amazon. So, why would a trillion-dollar corporation structure pay toward that outcome?

It's by design.

I believe Amazon structures salaries this way because it wants to retain employees who believe in the brand, who get behind the company's values, who believe in its leadership style, and who want to be part of something special. Employees who push past the twenty-four-month milestone are not staying for the money; they remain because—to their core—they believe in the company. People who leave would have left for money, so why not sift them out early, after a reasonable trial period? And new hires have a unique motivation to prove themselves. You're left with an organization filled with loyalty on one side, hustle on the other, and innovation where the two intersect.

Another innovation in forward-thinking organizations is establishing an environment that transcends a single mission statement. Traditional businesses often share metric targets with their employees. Their mission statement revolves around revenue thresholds, customer acquisition costs, or profit margins. When companies hit these numbers, it can leave employees asking, *What's next?* Continuing to hit numbers doesn't inspire employees. People want to know that their actions affect their larger community. Even if salaries fall short, employees who feel they're serving a higher purpose are more likely to stay.

Businesses like Amazon instil a principled mindset (sixteen principles, to be exact) and reinforce those principles in everything they do, from reports to daily communications. These principles reach different employees in different headspaces. If you don't yet have a personal or professional philosophy, you will likely absorb your company's philosophy. And if you already have a solid and principled ideology, you've probably already sought out an organization whose principles align with your beliefs. A well-articulated sense of greater purpose allows businesses to attract the right followers, cultivate passionate employees, and elevate focus to long-term gains.

Is this type of advanced innovation a suitable model for every start-up or corporation? No. But it's right for Amazon, and it works. Lest you think I may break out in song and dance over this structural model, now is probably the time for a quick reminder about mindset. Amazon is a trillion-dollar multinational corporation. It exists to innovate, but it also exists to sell products and please stockholders. When business is going well, Amazon hires like crazy; when business faces growth challenges, it restrategizes. A new strategy sometimes involves layoffs.

Once you understand and frame your mindset correctly, peace comes. Job security is lovely until it isn't. Job security likely means you're not learning new skills or getting the exposure you need to evolve. You may be overlooking opportunities. Professional growth follows disruption and innovation.

Traditional business practices exist because they work. The innovation side of the spectrum carries risk. Smart employees measure opportunities against this continuum, evaluate personal responsibilities and freedoms, look down the road at the trajectory of their industry, and make decisions accordingly.

The Intersection of Customers and Innovation

Our initial focus with AutoSahulat was registering mechanics to populate our web and Android platforms. After trying our service, one customer mentioned that he was more likely to use our services in the future if we offered value-added benefits.

The team took this feedback to heart. We brainstormed and devised a strategy to collaborate with various companies in the auto industry. We partnered with engine-oil companies, car-wash services, battery-replacement services, and periodic-maintenance providers to offer discounts to our customers. Specific codes for these discounts were redeemable through our app. This allowed customers to take advantage of the discounts and keep AutoSahulat at the forefront of their mind for any vehicle-related issue.

Pivoting based on the feedback of one customer is risky. Instinctively, it makes sense to wait until multiple sources of feedback circle around the same suggestion. However, that one customer could indeed suggest an idea that eventually becomes the lynchpin to your business's success. In these situations, having a diverse team with many perspectives is invaluable.

Before the pandemic, the Careem app expanded into bus service but suspended this part of ride-hailing during lockdowns. When employees began returning to work, one of our corporate customers approached us about starting a vanpooling service for female employees. They gave us a timeline of two months to launch the service, with a trial period of two weeks and no guarantee of a contract because we were new to the service. If the two-week trial went well, they promised to contract fifteen vans for one hundred employees.

When the van service started, we received feedback that our driver was not professional enough and his vehicle had not been sanitized to the passengers' satisfaction. The driver denied the claims. By the second time the service was called on, we had placed two vans on standby and asked one of our associates to be with the driver for the rest of the trial period, our way of addressing our customer's needs immediately. Ultimately, we got the contract, then added sedan service for company executives. Both services combined for a significant increase in revenue.

The goal was to determine as quickly as possible what customers wanted and what they'd pay for. Sometimes the product already exists, so you're innovating on what's out there. Rideshare was not new, but it disrupted the taxi industry. Google Maps did not invent maps but innovated people's access to them.

Entrepreneurs and company leaders who are willing to change their approach based on customer feedback are successful. At AutoSahulat, I took this strategy seriously. We were in daily discussions with our mechanics, asking them what they needed and getting them that help immediately, but something needed to be fixed on the customer side.

Founder Blindness

Founder blindness happens when a founder remains tightly attached to the original idea and disregards customer feedback and data. This state of mind poses a risk to the equilibrium between tradition and innovation.

AutoSahulat was not reaching the right customers. Although it's true that in Pakistan far more used vehicles are on the road than in developed countries, this tradition in the country seemed to be preventing our innovation: *You get to know mechanics over time and build a relationship. And, realistically, how many times does a car break down?* People who were close to me said it ate away at my confidence in our model until I, too, questioned it all.

We were haemorrhaging money. Customers and patterns kept changing. Something had to be done.

I held off until the office emptied in the late hours and only Mohsin and I remained, a situation reminiscent of our beginning. A rare downpour had drenched the previous hour. Our office door was propped open to the humid air. The scent of rain-soaked soil blended with the faint aroma of brewed tea. Distant honking and the shouts of street vendors finishing out their sales trickled in.

Mohsin sat, legs crossed, on a worn-out sofa we'd acquired from his family. Our start-up was lean, down to the chipped tiles beneath our feet. He flipped through printed reports that were pinched on a clipboard. I turned a wooden chair around and lowered myself, arms crossed over the ladder back.

"Moh—"

"Yeah, what's up?" He flipped a few more pages without looking up.

"Maybe it's time to look at something different."

He glanced at me and squinted. "What?"

I wasn't sure if his focus was split or if he was already on the defensive. I charged ahead.

"Or launch other products parallel to this model—something that can help us generate revenue to sustain."

Mohsin's lips parted as if I had suggested he have an affair behind the back of his first love. "No. Absolutely not." He tossed the clipboard aside and paced to the corner of the room to his anchor, his desk, but one that no longer shined with polish and the trappings of a start-up on the brink. He rifled page corners but didn't sit. It was so unlike him to waste energy. The guy was controlled, brilliant. "We need more cities." His wavering voice betrayed the easy confidence of a shoulder shrug.

"We don't have customers in the cities we're in, man. We're doing something wrong."

I fought standing. He was a full head and shoulders shorter than me, but I didn't want my size to play a role in our discussion. If anything, his passion for AutoSahulat diminished me.

"We have to show investors growth numbers," I said. "I think it's time to get into used cars."

The colour drained from his face. "No."

"It isn't that much of a stretch from where we are—"

"I didn't launch this start-up to become a used car salesman." His words popped off like a diesel engine when fuel hits hot exhaust. The only thing missing was smoke. He lowered himself to his desk chair.

Still, I pushed. I had staked everything on this too. "At this rate, we won't see the end of the year."

I was loud. Louder than I intended. I wanted to start the conversation over, to set the words loose in a way that was nothing like how Father would do it.

"We'll make it work." Mohsin's voice was bruised and quiet.

Too quiet. He didn't leave the office that day of the rain, so I did. I worried that I'd forced the end of the line.

We had three more arguments about the same topic—me pushing change; him holding steady to his vision. Eventually, I surrendered. Auto-Sahulat had been his idea.

I won't say this impasse is the reason we failed. For the longest time, blaming the regulatory systems that invited corruption was easier. But I recognized our division for what it was. I push. That's what I do. Saria's words—*You always do this to us. Are you crazy?*—had never rung truer. But if I pushed too hard, Mohsin held on too tightly to his original idea. His was a love affair. Founder blindness. I figured he had enough passion for both of us.

I was wrong.

Finding Your Equilibrium

Traditional business practices exist because they've withstood the test of time. Using them brings you credibility. Innovation moves you forward and helps you stand out in a crowded marketplace. Finding the right balance between the two is an ongoing journey for anyone in business. For outsiders who often face biases in the professional world, a balance of traditional and innovative approaches helps them better navigate barriers. To ensure you return to the equilibrium that's right for you, keep the following in mind:

> *Prioritize ethics.* Whether you're establishing a business or working as an employee of a larger entity, strive for fairness and integrity. Poor conduct does irreversible damage to your brand.
>
> *Support diversity.* Be the change you wish to see in business. An office with people who look like you, think like you, and have a similar background as you will not create a sustainable business.

Strengthen your foundation. You don't have to attend an Ivy League school (or any school, for that matter) to learn business fundamentals. Look for opportunities to learn the basics of marketing, accounting, finance, and strategy. Read widely and often. Dive into evergreen texts and current events.

Learn from the past. Immerse yourself in stories about other entrepreneurs and businesspeople, especially those who approached the industry from the outside in. Those who have cleared a path can offer valuable insights into navigating the sometimes harsh professional climate. Use these individuals as inspiration for your journey.

Network and seek out mentors. A strong network and quality mentors bring valuable knowledge and diverse experience to professional relationships. These are the individuals you will turn to when you feel off-balance. Nurture those connections. Give as much as you get.

Balance results from consistently choosing to do things with intention, as well as consistently choosing to live with intention. And balance requires a healthy respect for the traditional as well as a willingness to be bold. Balance also comes from within. Don't search for it when you cross business milestones—*when my start-up is fully funded, when the expansion is complete, when I'm finally hired at my dream corporation.* Those are external milestones. Balance is not found there.

There are some traditions I cannot let go.

I am not fully religious, but if I'm on an airplane and it takes a nosedive, I'll recite the Quran and become a devout Muslim right then. In moments when life seems out of control and my hope is depleted, I'll break free and walk a few steps into the sea, thinking God is out there. I'll feel the waves ripple at my feet and walk deeper, slowly, slowly, up to my neck.

I feel inescapably tied to my family-based roots. Saria and my kids are on a unique plane; my sun rises and sets with them. But my responsibility to my extended family, that sense of ancestry and history and community back in Pakistan, that is a complex tradition from which to untangle. When I return to my homeland, I feel like I should do more for my country, but I'm reminded of my frustration: the country's problems are manufactured, inevitable, given the antiquated mindset. I don't believe in agenda-driven patriotism, maps, or borders, but the boy inside me thinks I should. I am in a position to evoke change. *Real* change. Change that begins with the small start-up culture in Pakistan and has no end. And yet, I hesitate. Should I think of Saria and my kids and ignore the rest? Is it selfish to think of me?

Dad was foremost a military man who loaded his family with crates of eggs, but he gave me advice that I carry through my businesses, global travels, and dreams. About everything: *Move forward. Keep moving forward.* That is what he must have told himself when his brother ripped up those travel documents all those years ago. *Move forward.* Slow is still progress. Just like on a pastel-yellow bike, balance comes easier with momentum. *Keep moving forward.*

Maybe someday I'll disrupt Pakistani politics. There will be barriers. Sweets fallen to the dirt. I'd be perceived as a rule breaker, and people would misunderstand me for a stretch of time. But there is tradition, and there is innovation, and I've navigated the spectrum.

Move forward. A mix of the two is best.

7

EXPECT CHAOS

Saria asked me for a ride to the school that day. She was running late, and could I drop her off? Traffic was light. Though I did not see what was coming, I made a U-turn.

A car smashed into our passenger side.

She shouted my name. *Gullu!!!*

My face struck the steering wheel.

The mistake was on me. I might have killed her. I don't know how Saria survived the impact except to say she was wearing her seatbelt.

I was not.

I lost consciousness, though I can't say for how long. When I awoke, everything that had been inside our car was outside of it, and all that glass shattered into ten million pieces. A small crowd clustered and spoke to us and at us, though I could not process their words. Traffic flowed around our mid-sized sedan, now crushed to half its size.

A stranger scrambled to Saria's bag, plucked out her cell phone, and ran.

The guy saw an opportunity and took it.

I don't remember much about the accident and its aftermath, but in my bloody sideways view, I remember the thief.

These were the days of my fertilizer gig and some tough times. I was one week out of the hospital from my initial paralysis episode. I did not want to accept one more misfortune. My tears in the dented grey car had me thinking about life and its fragility.

We plan for months, years, and decades but never know tomorrow. We delude ourselves into thinking we have control, but one moment unravels so much. Best-laid plans travel through success milestones, points A to S—the *S* for success—points of basic education, then higher education, then advanced degrees, then internships, then first jobs, then supervisory roles . . .

All those points are a lie.

Few people agree with me on this.

There is no structure, only randomness.

And yet, outsiders look at A to S and exclude themselves before they have the luxury of a dream. Instead of embracing truths and telling their stories, they measure their worth against this lie.

Goals are strategic. Some argue that goals are paramount to success. But how to reach those goals? It cannot be a straight line. It's *never* a straight line.

I never shied away from telling others about my professional goals.

I want to work in big tech.

I want to start a start-up.

I want to raise substantial funding.

Almost always, I heard:

You don't have the academics.

You don't have the skill set.

You don't have the exposure.

And yet, I achieved all these things.

Start-ups are random and chaotic. Start-ups disrupt products, ideas, and entire industries. Start-ups do not follow the A to S of how things are *supposed* to be. By definition, start-ups *must* be different, so they are a good vessel for outsiders who continually beat the closed doors of refusals and wish to embrace the less-travelled paths of opportunity.

Chaos can be a catalyst for growth and business innovation. Your mindset and how you navigate chaos can make the difference between becoming an insider and languishing on the periphery.

Honking is just one symptom of chaos in Pakistan.

I've driven or been a passenger in a dozen other countries. No other culture lays on their car horns in traffic like Pakistanis. We have an intensity about reaching our destination as quickly as possible. Honking means *move.* Honking means *give me space.* Honking means *I'm coming over now* or *I need to move where you are.* Signals mean nothing. If you're not honking at others, you're not driving properly.

The constant noise is a zombie that eats your brain.

Another symptom of chaos back home in Karachi, a city I adore, is that most people carry two mobile phones—a real phone and a burner that won't wreck us if stolen. The real one we carry beneath layers, deep in pockets, in our bowels if we could. When wearable and insertable tech is fully realized, it will be huge there. Thieves on motorbikes won't be able to thread through crowds grabbing phones left and right. Or rifle through a victim's purse and snatch her mobile device after a car accident.

Widespread poverty and desperation lead people to such actions. Understandable, yet frustrating.

I have a friend named Mansoor who carries a hammer for protection.

One time, I asked him, "Why do you have this? A gun is a faster way to defend yourself."

Mansoor replied, "When I swing it over my head and scream, people will think I'm psychotic. So, I'm safe."

That kind of twisted logic makes sense in a twisted place like Pakistan.

It's sometimes difficult for insiders to understand that where you are born determines 70 percent of how your life will unfold. Westernized countries offer ample opportunities that aren't available in places like Pakistan. Exposure is everything. If no one in a child's environment has been exposed to opportunity, that child will not be part of the 30 percent who break out.

No matter what kind of chaos makes you an outsider, living in chaos is an opportunity. The most inspiring stories involve protagonists who push through adversity, overcome hardship, and persevere. Personal brand stories from outsiders are the best kind of different. Students, young professionals, marginalized populations, and older professionals, along with those from other developing nations, should leverage their version of chaos to create a narrative that invites the business world to enter, to learn, and to marvel at all that insiders don't know. That chaos shaped your journey in business and in life, and it's a tremendous asset. It accustoms you to the chaos inevitable in the business ecosystem.

The Business Side of Chaos

Truck art originated in Pakistan. Artisans known as *kamangars* use brightly coloured enamel paint to decorate the surfaces of trucks, buses, and other forms of transportation with elaborate patterns, traditional folk art, calligraphy, portraits, and scenes. In addition to being an eye-catching form of self- or business expression, truck art is believed to bring good fortune.

Truck art began in the 1920s, when it was used to add a protective coating to the Bedford commercial trucks the British brought to Pakistan. The tradition continued as a form of cultural pride and is now so popular that tens of thousands of artists make a living wage from their talents.

Visually, truck art is chaotic. Beautifully chaotic. Designs usually cover the entire vehicle and sometimes extend to the vehicle's interior and undercarriage. Almost no surface goes untouched. These masterpieces on wheels are a perfect metaphor for business disruption. One day, you're coasting on profits. The next day, an artistically designed Bedford truck of supply chain or technology or personnel or economic disruption rolls up on you, distracts you, thrusts you and everyone around you into chaos, and then rolls away, leaving you to deal with the aftermath.

AutoSahulat's truck art was regulatory chaos.

Disruptions are inherent to the business world. Entrepreneurs, founders, small businesses, and those who wish to work with them can thrive in uncertain times if a basic structure and an innovative mindset are in place:

> *Build a culture for innovation.* Create a flexible business culture that encourages proactive thinking, risk-taking, and learning from failures. Innovation will follow. Leaders who emphasize team building attract the strongest talent, and leaders who empower their teams retain that talent.
>
> *Remain agile.* Be open to new ideas. Reimagine existing ideas. Your willingness to pivot or switch gears entirely when disruption occurs is a predictor of how long it will take for you to bounce back from adversity.
>
> *Become customer obsessed.* Listen and respond to the ever-changing needs of your customers. You will realize that competition is a blessing when you adopt the mindset that customer feedback leads you to the place where you can thrive.
>
> *Assemble a strong network.* Build a network of mentors and peers in your industry and beyond who encourage the exchange of ideas, lend support, collaborate, and open their networks to you. Be a good steward of that network and do the same when others struggle.

> *Anticipate.* Disruption is a guarantee. Don't think in terms of rules; rules change in business. During calm times, consider potential disruptions and establish strategies for each scenario so that you can react quickly when uncertainty sets in.

In the early days of AutoSahulat, Mohsin and I knew we needed a call centre to assist customers who had difficulty reaching us via the web and app platforms. We opened a dedicated cell number, and then we each took fifteen-day shifts managing calls. One reason we did it this way was to understand better how we could improve the efficiency of real-time assistance for our customers. Another was cost. A proper call centre, between equipment and salaries, would have cost us thousands of dollars per month, whereas splitting the task between us two founders was nothing more than a monthly cell phone bill.

When I say founders wear many hats, well . . .

One evening around eight o'clock, I received a call from a customer with a dead battery. He needed ignition support and a replacement battery installed at his location. I searched through the database of registered mechanics nearest his location, assigned the one with the minimum estimated arrival time, and informed the customer the technician would be there within twenty to twenty-five minutes, our average response time.

After ten minutes, the mechanic called to say that his routes were blocked by a political procession. No other nearby mechanic wanted to deal with the political spectacle, so I hopped in my car, bought a battery, and paid a nearby mechanic some extra cash to meet me at the customer's location. The instance cost me far more than a typical transaction, but we ended up with a happy customer and a decent review.

The political parade was small-scale chaos (unless you consider the gross magnitude of politics in Pakistan). This was one customer on one day, but the process for handling disruption is the same with one customer as it is with a large-scale economic downturn. I pivoted our system, contacted my network for help, and executed a plan with that one customer at the core.

This level of customer obsession nearly always leads to lessons and ways to innovate.

The Employee Side of Chaos

As on the business end of chaos, much of chaos management on the employee side is perpetually undergoing transformation. As an employee, you may not make the most significant decisions related to the disruption of your employer's business, but you can put things in place to ensure you emerge stronger than ever.

> *Don't allow loyalty to hold you back.* To have value, longevity in employment must benefit both the employer and the employee. Working in different roles with different companies rapidly grows your skills. With the rate of technology evolving, even staying five years at one company leaves you at risk of stagnating while others in your field forge ahead.
>
> *Learn.* Innovate yourself. Unlearn and learn again. Take the initiative to expand your knowledge and skill set. Lean into new technologies. If your employer doesn't provide avenues for growth, seek them out independently. Everything you want to know is out there. You just have to find it and go for it.
>
> *Mind your mindset.* Maintaining a clear head and a positive attitude is critical. There is always a positive spin if you look hard enough. Focus on what you have instead of what you've lost. Understand that nothing is permanent and that failure presents an opportunity.

> *Conceptualize your brand.* Waiting until a crisis, such as a layoff, to figure out who you are and what you want is a quick road to a tangential dead end. Although it's true that adversity shines a spotlight on the important things in life, understand that who you settle into being when life is smooth is the most significant part of who you are.
>
> *Nurture your inner storyteller.* How you tell your story during times of chaos may differ from the narrative you typically share. That's okay. Communicating how you handle adversity makes the best kind of story. Be sure to take responsibility for your lessons learned and keep it positive. Your network will respond.
>
> *Embrace discomfort.* Take that opportunity that scares you. Be willing to be the dumbest person in the room.

Notice that I didn't advise you to work on your network during times of adversity. Chaotic periods are not the ideal time to grow your network. If you do, you have the potential to come across as desperate. This is the strategy most people use, and it doesn't work. You should continually grow your network instead of just during challenging times.

One of the biggest disruptors in the future of business in nearly every industry will be AI. In the not-so-distant future, entire degreed professions may be at risk of extinction in much the same way that manufacturing jobs disappeared when automation came along. How to weather this particular and monumental chaos? Innovate yourself. AI likely won't replace your profession—at least in your lifetime—but it *will* replace those who refuse to use AI as a tool to grow inside their profession. So continuously seek self-improvement, adapt to new technologies and methodologies, and reinvent your skills and knowledge to stay relevant in an ever-changing world.

Whatever difficult choices you face as an employee, make them yourself.

The worst failure is realizing you failed because you listened to someone else. That kind of influence does not promote self-awareness, reflection, and growth. Aim for paths where you, alone, will be blamed if things go south. Inside massive chaos is a masterclass in evolution.

Time is the ultimate chaos we experience. It's an insidious and ravenous thief. When I go through a challenging time, I think back to that dented grey car. The cursing and the tears. How, despite having just been laid off, despite the pain, I would give anything to go back to that day. When you find your life in chaos, it helps to tell yourself that in ten or twenty years, you would give anything to be going through what you're going through now, even if only to beat the clock's forward momentum.

Chaos, in business and in life, can be the ultimate catalyst for growth and innovation. So much of our journey is beyond our control, but you have agency over how you think and react.

"You have to stop," Saria said. "It's a scam."

"We've come this far." A million Pakistani rupees far. "Let's give just a little more money to see what happens."

I push. That's what I do.

We had sold our car on the promise of leaving Pakistan. Documents and free-and-clear immigration to Canada, or so we thought.

"This is just like before." Saria roamed the house, wringing her hands. The light left her eyes. I knew how she felt. I was an outsider in my country, and I couldn't leave.

I sat her down and held her folded hands in mine. "I won't let that happen to us again."

But, of course, I did. And I had.

Five years earlier, we sold the dowry she'd brought into our marriage—expensive jewellery—on the promise of a work visa for the United Kingdom. And there, in Pakistan, we still sat.

"If it doesn't work, we'll try for Australia. There's an immigration consultant in Karachi—"

"Stop," she whispered. "No more. The hope . . . it hurts too much."

We lived too far from the ocean to break free, to walk a few steps into the sea, and to believe that anything waited beyond for us. We would feel no waves at our feet; we would not walk deeper, slowly, slowly, up to our necks.

My dream of working for big tech was no secret. At each waystation of mentorship, at each start-up, at each place where I was invited to give a speech, my answer to the *What is your next step?* question was big tech. I wanted that experience on my résumé. For years, I had applied—Google, Microsoft, Apple, Netflix, Amazon, and countless others. I watched the people they hired and the teams they built. I wanted to get in as early as possible and be part of it all.

At one point, I blew an interview with a sales manager because an incoming call interrupted and dropped our cell connection. When the discussion resumed, I was distracted and off my focus—totally on me. Another time I was short-listed, and so I prepped for final interviews on the basis of one projected job opening. However, I discovered during the interview that they were looking to fill a completely different position. During my feedback, they said, *We're sorry you experienced this miscommunication.*

One day, years later, I logged onto social media. Someone at Amazon had reached out to me via private message.

It's a scam, I thought. I was conditioned into a state of perpetual defensiveness. I double-checked. Triple-checked. Cyber-investigated the man who reached out to me.

He was legit.

The invitation to talk about an opening hit out of the blue but not at all. I had applied to Amazon many times in the past. The lesson here crashes like a wave: Don't lose hope. *Keep moving forward.*

I kept the interview process to myself for six months because I didn't want Saria to be hurt again. When I got the job at Amazon in Malaysia, I showed her the offer email and held her folded hands in mine.

"An interview?" she asked.

"No, Saria. A job."

She blinked her beautiful eyes, withdrew her hands, and left for the office. I understood that volcanoes run deep, are inherently warm, and shape the landscape. Midmorning, she bombarded me with texts.

What does this mean?

Do we have to say goodbye to each other again?

We just moved the kids a year ago.

I'm afraid.

We had to renew our passports, including those of our children, but told them this was for a vacation to Turkey. We sold our belongings but did not tell our extended family until days before we left. We were conditioned into a state of perpetual defensiveness that did not dissipate until we were physically in Kuala Lumpur.

At one point in the final Amazon interview that had landed me the job, they asked, *Why Amazon?* I spoke about genuine things like exposure, culture, and vision. And then, I remembered my brand and became a storyteller.

I said that a company like Amazon, which is hyper-attuned to its global customer base, requires the right people to deliver on that principle. Global people. People who know what it's like to share an idea and risk retaliation but to do it anyway for the greater good. People who appreciate a work environment where independent thinking is honoured inside a group. I said those people should feel safe taking risks and be cared for and trained to become the best of the global talent pool.

I told them I could find those global people because I was one of them.

As I write this, Amazon has sent me to a new territory. I've never been to this territory before. I don't speak the language. The currency notes are crazy-high numbers that force me into a long mental pause to calculate the conversion.

On my taxi trip from the airport to the hotel, a traffic officer pulled my driver over. After a brief exchange, the taxi driver slipped the officer a few crisp bills. The officer then turned his attention to the back seat and asked me something I didn't understand.

My brain barely stopped moving through the article I was reading. I was conditioned into a state of perpetual defensiveness.

"How much do I have to pay?" I asked in English.

He strung together more insistent words. We volleyed questions back and forth until two things were abundantly clear: he hailed from a part of his country where loud was authoritative, and he had no intention of letting us go until I did a necessary transaction.

I sighed and showed him my wallet filled with the currency I had converted at the airport—20,000, 50,000, and 100,000 notes. "Man, just take it out. Take what you need."

The remainder of the way to the hotel was a long mental pause to calculate how much I'd given him. When I arrived at a number, a curse slipped out.

I might as well have been back in Karachi.

8

POUR TEA

"I can't figure out my life, man."

Saroosh was younger, twenty-four or so. He was handsome in the way that all youth are and in that fearless way that propels him into trying new things. His full-tooth grin stretched to both earlobes and reminded me of the Dentonic tooth powder cartoon advertisements that used to run on Pakistani television when I was a kid. He carried the burdens of a man twice his age, but you'd never know it. He was as grounded as an acacia tree, with a similar umbrella-like crown of dark hair.

"You have time," I said.

Most nights, we sat on the roof and drank unlawful things. In Karachi, fewer people cared about the forbidden. Diversity in the southern part of the country made such things accepted and dangerous. Public drinking made you a criminal, but everyone did it privately. Peak Pakistanian hypocrisy.

"You've always had good instincts," Saroosh said. "Tell me what to do next."

"What's wrong with where you are? You're already working remotely. Canadian dollars, man."

He shook his head and stared off at the flickering city lights, a stark contrast to our darkness. Our Singaporean landlord had strict criteria for his rentals here—professionals only—but his standards ended there. The rooftop was nothing but broken furniture and incinerated plants.

"I feel like I've already lived a century. Like I'm looking back, and I can't breathe." He took a long, ambitious drag of his cigarette. "I just bought that car, the first real thing I've gotten for myself, and Father won't speak to me."

His father was not so different from my father. Both military. Both relentlessly pushing from behind. In Saroosh's case, it made sense. The guy was a whiz. With his academic potential, unlike mine at his age, he'd landed a scholarship to study at the Institute of Business Administration, a top university in Karachi, took on advanced trainings in search engine optimization, and logged freelance hours at several local start-ups. His father pushing him meant significant enhancements for his parents and two siblings.

"The car benefits everyone."

"Yeah, well, he doesn't see it that way."

"You should go somewhere."

Saroosh's chuckle was loose, already intoxicated. "Right."

"No, I mean it. Get a visa. Just go somewhere. Anywhere. Expose yourself to something new."

"Not everyone has a Saria."

I knew what he meant. She was understanding beyond belief. The day I told her I had to move to Singapore for two months to attend a program—that if I received funding for my start-up, it would be a dream come true, but if that didn't happen, I would still be building a network and good things would come of it—was the day she resigned herself to living with risk. Risk meant working to fill my income gaps, being an emotional port in my storms, and sometimes living apart—like me being in Karachi, without her.

"You have a job," I said. "You can work from anywhere. Why stay here under your father's rules? So long as the money comes home, he cannot have an opinion about what he doesn't know."

The filter at the end of Saroosh's shortening cigarette blinked orange and crackled. Smoke curled upward, visible only by our crescent moon over the desert. "I'm not like you, man. My instincts aren't there. You told me to leave that start-up months before it went under. You said it was no good, and I didn't listen. Every time I reached out to people on social media, it was all wrong . . ."

I laughed. "You *were* obnoxious. Telling chief marketing officers at global companies that they were doing SEO wrong. I had to say something."

"What if I get somewhere and don't know what to do?"

"Would you be in any different position than where you are now?" I emptied my glass and poured another for us both. "If nothing comes of it, you will have breathed. And that is how you figure out life. You breathe."

He extinguished the cigarette against his boot sole and sighed.

"Besides, you have my number," I said. "I have no problem telling you you're wrong from anywhere in the world."

A week later, Saroosh peppered my door with knocks. Before I could swing it fully open, he bounded in. His smile was as radiant and blinding as the snow-capped peak of K2, the second-highest mountain in the world. "I'm going to Bali."

"What?"

"I found a hostel. For three months, I'm going to live there."

"Sounds perfect. Send me pictures so I can be jealous."

We shook hands. I would miss our talks.

He confided his nervousness. I told him the greater risk to his happiness was staying and doing nothing.

Over the next weeks, Saroosh sent me photos of caves and shamans and friends from Bali. New friends. Friends from all over the world, taking a spiritual trek together. He gushed about how cheap it was to be there. Living like royalty in Bali was possible, even if the only skill he possessed was to teach English to the children of wealthy locals. He plugged into the freelance ecosystem and learned how people grew and evolved outside the walls of an institution. And he learned to swim. When his time in Bali was up, he returned to Karachi. He had connected with people who held degrees from Oxford and had begun a start-up.

Networking made all the difference for Saroosh. He went from his nuclear family and close social circle of elite IBA graduates who believed they already knew everything to being part of a vibrant freelance and entrepreneurial community. A global community.

He found the courage to embrace discomfort.

He found space to breathe.

Pakistanis are excellent hosts. We treat guests like kings and queens. No one who darkens our door goes without food or drink.

My position exposes me to people from many different cultures. When we meet, I'm amazed that they ask for little beyond a glass of water. Join me in Pakistan, and we'll have sodas and desserts. We'll talk about things that have nothing to do with business. We'll ask about your family and want you to bring them along. We'll bring our families too. Sometimes it is perceived as going overboard, but culturally, we crave interaction and see outsiders as a blessing.

If only the rest of the world did the same.

We are forthcoming with our intentions in business and beyond. If I help you with something, you, someone else, or God, will help me in some way. If I invest time or knowledge, time or knowledge will return to me. The mindset is a bit karma-driven, a bit of a by-product of placing extreme value on the human connection.

One of my strengths in business is sales. We've heard that to succeed in business, we must build relationships first, conduct business second. Sometimes I get so preoccupied with the first, I never end up selling anything—at least not initially. Instead, I get to know the people I encounter. I gain insights into what they think about. I assist or sometimes just lend a sympathetic ear. I open up to them. In turn, they open up to me. We become kings and queens in each other's spheres. And there may be a sale or two in there, as well.

It's strange, coming at this as the boy who hid in the back of the classroom and put a bridge between himself and the rest of the world. Maybe somewhere along the way, I figured out the *Roshan-e-Pul* was only magnificent in scope and light when there were people to enjoy it with me.

Networking is building and nurturing connections with others—individuals, professionals, and organizations. You're already networking if you're going out, meeting people, and doing your work. Next-level networking, both in person and online, is what bridges the gap between being an outsider and being an insider. Every time I failed, every time I started from zero, my network came through for me. I had people to reach out to. They already knew me through my branding and storytelling, and they remembered me. And if they didn't know these things, they likely knew someone in our shared network who did know these things about me.

The hard-core things about business—spreadsheets, presentations, funding, communication, and software—all adapt and progress based on trends, perspectives, and tech. This lessens their importance in the grand scheme. You will forever spend your days replacing old tools with new tools, so resist targeting this for meaningful growth. The desire for and practice *of* authentic human connection, however, remains constant.

An ideal network achieves organic growth through diversity—not just of people but also of experiences. If the only people you see daily for five or ten years are the same handful of corporate team members, your network remains small and closed. Not only will changing jobs bring you professional growth, but moving into a new role at a different entity also expands your network. And if those jobs involve going out and meeting new people, that growth is exponential.

When layoffs come, would you rather be part of a handful or part of the exponential?

Networking isn't about being charismatic or extroverted. Introverts are often gifted at communication because they listen more than they talk and don't mind shining the spotlight on others. Some of the most influential and magnetic people in my network are introverts. No matter your comfort level with networking, you will build quality connections that endure if you approach people from a place of authenticity. Treat those in your network like kings and queens. Invite them for a virtual chat. Become so preoccupied with building a relationship that you forget to ask anything of them.

I fall to the extroverted side of networking. I love attending parties. I love to travel. Bonding at a retreat is one of my favourite ways to build professional relationships. Going to a different setting to wind down with others, even if it's just a bite to eat after work, is when I most come alive. My brand reflects these truths about me. I couldn't always afford to do these things, but there are budget-friendly ways to achieve the same networking outcome.

When I lived in Karachi, in the flat next to Saroosh, I fully embraced the nightly cultural tradition of drinking chai at outdoor cafés. The price of a cup of tea or flaky pastry bought you admittance to the grapevine of community news, a wealth of advice from those who had navigated life's challenges for decades longer, and the infectious optimism of a young and vibrant scene. I'd invite whomever I met during my daily tasks to join me every Thursday and Friday evening at my favourite spot. I'd leave it low-key: *I'll be there, come and meet me if you want.* I was surprised how often people showed up. We'd talk about anything and everything. Sometimes we discussed business, but I aimed to get to know them as people first and potential industry connections second.

In retrospect, I spent many of those hours mentoring young professionals like Saroosh. They printed out their résumés, and we would go over them together. I'd suggest changes. I introduced them to people who needed their skill sets. We scrolled through their social media platforms and ensured that what they posted told the world the right personal story. Their perspectives were refreshing, and they gave me hope for the future.

I benefited from these nights in the cafés, too. When friends who worked at different companies shared what was happening in their business or industry; it was a mighty flood of market intelligence to help me make decisions in my sphere. And the next week, they often brought their colleagues, so my network expanded rapidly. I worked on personal branding and fine-tuned my storytelling. Those six hours or so per week were a time investment well spent.

This model of networking is not limited by geography. With a solid internet connection, a camera on your device, a shared language, and a drive to make it happen, you can set up a mastermind-style group that exposes participants to world trends and cultures. Topics such as referrals, collaborations, mentoring, venture capitalist opportunities, industry trends, and access to knowledge and resources that can be discussed locally take on a whole different perspective when shared globally.

As an outsider, key into niche communities, forums, and platforms that cater to your uniqueness. Use these safer avenues to build your networking confidence, then branch out to diverse platforms. Engage in discussions and participate in virtual events. Share your story online in an engaging way. Remember, what makes you different also makes you memorable.

Look for Opportunities

I recently received an email about an inspirational event happening in Malaysia that coincided with the period I would be in the country. They were looking for speakers and included a link. Within minutes and without much thought, I clicked through, filled out the form, and submitted myself for consideration. The next day, I was added as a speaker.

Most people would have deleted the email. Or skimmed the form and not submitted or attended, let alone volunteered to be a speaker.

Mini opportunities to network are often more important than large-scale events. Smaller interactions allow me to put my brand and story in front of people who may not normally hear it. Small opportunities tend to come along more often and allow me to be remembered as a bigger fish in a smaller pond. People at small events are less intimidated and more likely to open up and connect without the pressures of bigger players in attendance.

In the case of the Malaysia event, the organizers promoted it on social media. Reposting their publicity gave me valuable content for my social media. Volunteering to help motivate others fits nicely with my brand. My boss saw the post and asked about it. I said, "There are a few people I hope to connect with there, and I'm happy to help others when possible."

Reality manifests the dreams we put into action. If you hope to inspire people someday, find your inspirational story and put it out there. If you wish to be a bestselling author one day, learn to write and put yourself out there for those who aren't as far along in their journey. If you want to be a world traveller, find ways to travel locally and gather a network that supports your dreams—or jump into the deep end of the ocean as Saroosh did in Bali.

Small opportunities cross your awareness every day. Instead of tuning them out or deleting them, consider how a mini event might advance your goals.

The Right Way to Reach Out

As a nobody from a developing nation, I have been on the low end of the networking spectrum. As someone who realized his dreams of working in big tech, traveling the globe, and meeting venture capitalists, I have also been on the pursued end of the networking spectrum. There is a right way and a wrong way to navigate these encounters.

At the risk of sounding cliché, you want to leave others better than when you found them. This is especially important when approaching those with industry clout. This is not about false sentiments or floating egos. Flattery is obvious and vacant and turns others off. As someone with less authority or influence, you can make a difference for that better-connected individual by acknowledging and appreciating their contributions, promoting them, or promoting something they're passionate about, offering and aiding in completing tasks in areas that showcase your strengths, sharing their successes on social media, and fostering connections to your network that may be of use to them. Sometimes what people need the most is someone to listen to them and allow them to blow off steam.

Connecting authentically takes months. Years. You're interacting for long-term relationships, not short-term gains.

Encounters should not be agenda driven. Enter conversations with the mindset that nothing will ever come of it—*and that's okay*. Even if you don't get the opportunity to share your brand or your story, no connection is ever wasted and that is because you're still learning.

I often hear *I follow you on social media*. This statement is usually chased with something like *You're doing a marvellous job in the tech sector*. Sometimes they'll add a clapping emoji.

Please don't add emojis.

What does that mean? *What* am I doing in the tech sector that's so marvellous? Instead, pinpoint something that inspires me to listen to you. Tossing out a statement and failing to follow it up with something meaningful is disingenuous and a waste of time.

Remember, when conversing with people in their forties and fifties, these individuals have at least fifteen to twenty years of experience in the business sector and a history of interacting with thousands of people at different talent levels and with different backgrounds. Understand and accept that they will judge you at first encounter because they have experience. Start on the right foot. Tell them something they may not be aware of or something that may surprise them. If you mention something that snags their thoughts or causes them to question their beliefs, they will remember you.

And your aim is to be remembered.

The Aged Outsider

A CFO named Ali at a pesticide company in Pakistan was laid off a few years ago. He opened a legal firm that helps start-ups navigate problematic laws and regulations. When he reached out to me to ask if we could meet, it was an automatic yes from me. In my mind, he is a senior-level executive with experience, resources, and a seasoned network in place. The pesticide company's loss is certainly everyone else's gain.

I approached the encounter as an opportunity to learn and connect with someone new. If no business materialized from it, that was okay. I connected Ali with a few start-ups and encouraged him to attend upcoming networking events. He was there, at the events, handing out his business card. People listened to what he had to say because he had achieved so much in his previous role.

If you face job transition at an advanced age and believe you're being overlooked for opportunities, you're in a unique networking position. You may have substantial connections in place, but your network may be tired, filled with professional relationships you haven't nurtured, or in an industry that has been slow to embrace innovation. Even in your late thirties to fifties, you will level up by setting goals, advancing your knowledge, and constructing that personal brand. Rather than reaching out to junior or midlevel industry people, your age gives you the advantage of reaching out to individuals in senior-level positions.

Start with your existing network. Because they know, like, and trust you, they can introduce you to many people—a secondary network. Especially if you have experienced gap years because of retirement or a job venture that didn't work out, be willing to accept less salary or a position adjacent to what you want to do. Use this time to enhance your skills and grow your network in new directions. No learning is ever wasted. Appreciate your professional and personal history and leverage it into your brand to become a great storyteller. People will listen.

Your Board of Advisors

Every mentor has strengths. Some excel with spreadsheets and ledgers. Some are rock stars at networking or securing investments. Others have soft skills or are masterful at navigating a healthy balance between their personal and professional lives. No individual can be everything you need as a mentor, nor should you ask someone to fill all those roles. It's time to rethink the idea of a solitary mentor and shift attention to a collection of people who advise you based on their strengths.

A board of advisors.

We all have people we go to for advice in distinct areas of our lives. You probably already have a board of advisors, though you may not have thought of them in that light. Unlike a traditional board of advisors in the business sense, your board might not know each other. Even separately, their capacity to advise and challenge you to be your best is invaluable.

Your best board of advisors begins when you consider your goals and needs. Zero in on areas where you'd like support. Before you pick someone, determine the criteria that make someone a solid choice as a mentor. Starting your search with clarity ensures you'll find the best fit.

As you consider your network, ask yourself if anyone fits your desired parameters. Pay close attention to individuals with diverse experiences or a background that you do not share. Robust and thought-provoking discussions happen when the chasm between mentor and mentee is generous but respectful. Note gaps in your existing network and make special efforts to grow your connections in deficit areas.

Pay close attention to people's successes. Just because you have a friendly rapport with someone doesn't mean that person is a good fit for your advisory board. You need mentors who have experienced wins in your industry. Age shouldn't necessarily be a factor, but longevity in your field equates to a richness and breadth of experience and valuable connections.

Be mindful of their time. Even if you meet infrequently, you must trust that when you need advice, an individual will make time for you. Don't expect mentors to remain on your board forever. As in personal relationships, there is a season for professional mentorships. Honour these connections while you have them but recognize when they've run their course.

Trust in your mentors is a factor that cannot be understated. Especially when considering individuals in your network, you must be confident that what you discuss remains sacred. Desire for confidentiality should be a talking point in early discussions with a potential mentor.

You may be asked to be on someone else's board of advisors. Be generous. Helping others is a gift that comes back around. You may even become part of your mentor's board. Reciprocating with advice creates a strong bond because you enter the relationship on an equal footing. If you go this route, however, beware that a breakdown in the mentorship results in a loss on both sides.

The demise of AutoSahulat taught me several important lessons. I fully realized the power of strong connections in business. They are especially crucial in developing nations prone to inconsistent, fluctuating, and sometimes corrupt systems. One of the other start-ups in the mobility sector left Pakistan about the time we closed AutoSahulat. The founders were from Egypt and contacted us to see if we could help them with regulation barriers. We wanted to help but lacked the influence and background to even save ourselves. Mohsin and I, and this Egyptian company, might have successfully navigated the regulatory issues with the right connections.

I also learned that the right team takes ownership and is more important than the idea or business model. Even if your board of advisors isn't part of your official team, you'll need the guidance of those mentors during times of crisis.

In all instances, listen more than you talk. We were created with two ears and one mouth, so approach the world with that mindset.

When I was with Careem, a university student reached out to me one day through social media. He had done a deep dive on one of our products. Full analytics. Data to back up his theory. And he followed that up with suggestions: *If you tweak it like this, you can increase the order volume by X amount . . .*

I brought this analysis to one of the directors who was looking into this food business. We worked through the math. Everything checked out.

Blew. My. Mind.

Not only had this individual demonstrated his skills—demonstrated, not bragged about—but he also had the courage to network in such a positive, helpful, and engaging way. And at such a young age.

The director and I got him on a call. The student impressed us so much that we offered him an internship.

In a similar way, around 2017, I engaged with a general manager at another company via social media on the topic of cryptocurrency. At the time, he had a massive interest in crypto and shared his thoughts on the subject online. Bitcoin was fluctuating like crazy, so there was much to discuss. Although digital currency wasn't a topic I knew a great deal about at the time, I researched and read widely on the subject in order to bring educated thoughts to our interactions. Fast-forward to the moment I showed an interest in working for his business. When I applied, he remembered me as the crypto guy. He didn't know much about my start-up or the products we sold, but that was okay. I had made an impression. Everything that came later was built on that healthy and respectful exchange of ideas on a topic he was passionate about.

I got the job.

That's how I was hired at Careem in 2019.

When it comes to making inroads in business, networking plays a more important role than the traditional elements professionals have typically led with, such as degrees, experience, and meticulous résumés. Paper diplomas don't make connections. People make connections. And that puts outsiders who prioritize networking at an advantage. If you are out there and people recognize you, you will be short-listed for opportunities. If people feel like they know you, if they remember you, they will bypass hiring algorithms to engage with you at the next level.

Every organization is constantly looking for people who add value to their company. Start-ups, especially, look for high performers.

In this book, I've spent quite a bit of page real-estate convincing you that what makes you an outsider is your superpower. And it is. It's also rough out there. You will run up against ugly individuals who make snap judgments based on ignorance and past experiences that have nothing to do with you. Outsiders must work harder to be seen. But you will be seen if you network the right way.

Focus on your skill set. Generate conversations around those strengths so that people remember you. Create posts on professional platforms about these topics. Be helpful. Read the posts of others on similar topics and comment in meaningful ways. Keep interacting with those posts—not just liking but commenting to build a conversation. Engaging conversations build relationships.

When you've finished reading this book, I invite you, my reader, to my virtual outdoor café. We'll have chai or a pastry and get to know each other first as people. Tell me *your* story. Even if nothing comes of it, we will have breathed.

No connections are ever wasted.

9

BE GENEROUS

My youngest brother, Nasir, and I occupied the same room as kids. We took primitive steps into independence together. A mutual pre-occupation with computers and doom-metal music was only the beginning.

He was the *rangoli* of the family—the vibrant and colourful centre point around which the family's patterns and rituals circulated. Even today, his predisposition for late nights and late-morning meals is the clockface around which the family turns. He's trusting and affectionate and inspires a fierce protective streak in those closest to him.

Fifteen years ago, Nasir pulled up to our place in his brand-new Honda Civic. Just off the showroom floor, the newest model was a rare sight. He had upgraded it with a sports kit and various modifications. Our inaugural road trip from Multan to Lahore was 330 kilometres of surround sound, new-car scent, and air-conditioning cold enough to form icicles on our beards.

Bliss.

When we reached Lahore, Nasir suggested we take the car to an auto shop. He wanted a few features checked because he was unfamiliar with how it handled the road, and he still had that residual anxiety of a new car owner. He pulled into the shop's bay behind a motorcycle parked for repair and got out to speak to the mechanic.

I climbed behind the wheel.

Nasir had driven the entire four-hour trip, so I hadn't yet experienced the ride from the driver's seat. The silky grey leather of the steering wheel, the electric-blue dashboard lights, and the digital speedometer at eye level were all unreal. I fiddled with lights, turned on indicators, window buttons, and ventilation knobs.

The mechanic told me to start the vehicle. I turned the ignition. The engine whispered to life.

Nasir and the mechanic stood beside the front passenger-side tire. Something beneath the propped-open hood drew their attention. They conferenced a while, then stood back to discuss. Nasir pointed to the back tire.

The mechanic walked along the car toward the rear bumper. He wiped his hands on a rag, whistled to get my attention, and hollered, "Press the brake."

I pressed the pedal.

It was not the brake.

The car lurched forward. My brain short-circuited. I mashed any pedal my foot could find. Wheels spun out. Metal crunched. Gas. Brake. Gas. The hood slammed shut. Men shouted.

I had driven up and over the motorcycle in the bay.

Pakistani men are not predisposed to crying. I thought for sure my brother would make an exception that day. The Civic's front end looked like a crushed soda can. We had to pay damages to the motorcycle owner. Nasir kept saying that it was okay, that at least no one was hurt, but I knew he was rethinking not putting a pillow over my face in my sleep when we were kids.

To lighten the mood, we called our friend Abbas Shah, whom we affectionately called Shah-*g*. Emphasis on the *g* because the guy was cool and hilarious. He wore bottle-bottom glasses and could mimic any noise. Human voices were his specialty. Shah-g pulled up in his puke-white Mehran and cracked jokes about the irony of the crappiest ride in Pakistan being the one to rescue passengers from a new Honda.

His jokes at my expense that day were brutal. Well-deserved but brutal. He treated us to dinner and dropped us off at our hotel. The Mehran peeled out around the corner. Shah-g's laughter backfired out the open window.

"I'm sorry, man." I'd lost count of how many times I apologized that evening.

"You owe me." Nasir scowled. "Maybe for eternity."

He never collected. That was just his way.

Nasir helped me out financially through my struggling years. In the same way that Pakistani parents hide things from their children, the Iqbal siblings protected each other's secrets from our parents. If there is such a thing as generosity to a fault, Nasir is guilty. Younger brothers are supposed to learn from their older brothers. In our case, Nasir reminds me that generosity is an expression of love.

And there is room for that in business.

Generosity goes beyond charity or material giving. Certainly, incorporating money-oriented outreach as part of your business philosophy is admirable. But gifts of your time, your ideas, your resources, and your passions have the potential to transcend any financial transaction and make a significant difference in the lives you touch.

Six months into my time with Careem, I noticed our sales numbers had stagnated. I suspected the reason was our decentralized structure. I managed our central region with four salespeople on my team. Other managers with teams of similar sizes took northern and southern territories. Motivation had also taken a hit.

Innovation does not come without pushback. Had I merely suggested an alternative structure, resistance would have come from all sides—management and salespeople—that is, if anyone really listened at all. Overcoming the inertia of such an entrenched system would be like trying to relocate the Badshahi Mosque with two toothpicks and a prayer. For my idea to be taken seriously, I needed to put in the work.

I devised a centralized structure that collected the company's entire sales team into one unit. I gathered anonymous evidence that regional teams were competing and hiding leads from each other so that their numbers would appear higher than others'. I crunched the data from the past months and quarters. I studied our portfolio and realized it had remained largely unchanged. We were not onboarding companies or innovating to respond to customer demands. I prepared my argument: approaching sales from a country-wide perspective results in a collaborative effort, where best practices are shared, new ideas and collective brainstorming ignite innovation, and motivation to work toward a common goal elevates everyone.

"Working in silos has gotten us nowhere," I concluded in my passionate presentation at the next internal meeting. "Let's come together under a single head and work toward a common goal."

General managers from across Pakistan exchanged glances and frowned as if I had suggested we package our products in garbage and float them down the Jhelum River.

At the following three internal meetings, I presented new data and angles about why centralizing the structure would be a good move. It wasn't until year-end numbers fizzled that they agreed to try my proposal. My line manager became head of sales, and I gave him my full support to ensure the new system succeeded.

Our unified team realized great outcomes. The interaction between regions resulted in shared leads and increased gross merchandise values. Careem's for-business portfolio saw a significant percentage increase in year-over-year growth, and we launched several new features based on customer and team feedback. Eventually, I was promoted to lead the team.

Leadership and Generosity

The best leaders are generous leaders.

Leadership isn't a plaque on the door or a nameplate on a desk. It doesn't walk onstage to loud applause or have a designated parking space closest to the company entrance. In many conventional organizations, once individuals advance into senior management roles, the hierarchy is designed to treat leaders as godlike entities.

Supervisors may block the growth of those they oversee, especially in places like Pakistan, where job insecurity is rampant. If employees are not growing or being mentored in a way that enables them to replace their supervisor, then that supervisor will never be replaced. It's a corrupt system of self-preservation designed to hold employees back.

Thankfully, that outdated culture is changing. Whereas, in days gone by, teams were expected to adhere to the wishes of a few central leaders, today's work climate champions individuals and asks those in authority to remain flexible with the talent they hire. Businesses and organizations increasingly want people in key positions to step into responsibility with the mindset of a team facilitator.

This is a unique and challenging role for leaders. Every team member has different talents, inspirations, goals, demands on their time, and thresholds for adversity and evolution.

Leaders who excel at strategizing and coordinating such a diverse array, who listen respectfully and act with integrity, are rewarded with vibrant and collaborative workplaces that elevate the success of all.

This type of leadership requires individuals to embody a spirit of generosity.

Generosity of ideas, resources, and opportunities goes beyond kindness. Whereas anyone in the work environment can exhibit a gift-giving mindset, those who step up and into special leadership roles are responsible for a special kind of generosity.

Creating true leaders is the ultimate shortcut to growth. Are you at risk of being replaced by those you lead? Sure. You might create wicked-smart monsters and put yourself out of a job. But that says more about you not innovating yourself than it says about them. And maybe if that happens, it's time for an exit to new challenges anyway.

Generosity for Individuals

When everyone was in lockdown during the COVID-19 pandemic, the ride-hailing industry, like many others, came to a grinding halt. I was shuttered in my house with my family, and I was bored. I wanted to do what I could to help others. Experience had taught me hard lessons. If I communicated the things that had worked for me, they might work for others. So, I made a list of topics I felt confident talking about and asked Zaina, my daughter, to record me on my cell phone.

The first videos were truly awful.

I listened to feedback from colleagues and learned how to edit. Slowly, my content evolved. Topics expanded and branched out. The video quality increased because I bought a camera. Angles and lighting became friendlier. Throughout this expedition of mine, my son, Ibrahim, and Zaina took the helm as directors, providing me with guidance. GuzPro is a YouTube channel aimed at a Pakistani audience, so it's a mix of Urdu and English, but it was a way for me to give back at a time when life delivered a major disruption that left us all feeling helpless.

My intent never was to monetize the content. Even today, many people reach out hoping that I will mentor them for a fee. That zone isn't for me. When people monetize their generosity, it's easy for them to lose purpose. Then, generosity is no longer pure of spirit.

Generosity in a workspace takes many forms.

- You can offer emotional support to colleagues who are going through a difficult time.

- Find reasons and ways to celebrate the achievements of others.

- Begin a social initiative or program that gives back to the community.
- Volunteer alongside colleagues for causes they feel passionate about.
- Share your expertise in a topic by teaching free seminars within your organization and beyond.
- Temporarily take on tasks that aren't yours to lessen someone's burden.
- Mentor someone.
- Pass along resources and opportunities.

None of these involve money.

Another way to spread generosity is to share your story. If you have a history and truth that can aid or inspire others going through challenges, consider sharing your story on a larger scale. This vulnerability, this putting yourself out there, requires courage, but that heart is your *sohan halwa*, a delicacy. Audiences are wildly perceptive. So long as you come to the project with a mindset of generosity, you will connect and inspire.

Individuals who act in generous ways are at an advantage in corporations; this is because time is the one commodity that a large entity cannot easily give away. Use the power of one to lift others. Generosity has a ripple effect. Kindness inspires and spreads.

Generosity in Business

People are drawn to ecosystems of generosity.

But generosity is rarely discussed in business terms. After all, the end goal is to make more money than the competition. However, a culture of generosity in business yields significant benefits for individuals and organizations in these areas:

> *Customer feedback:* The most valuable business insights come from gaining a deeper understanding of customer

needs. That means caring about the things your customers care about and actively engaging your customers, even if it costs more time and money to forge that relationship. Customer obsession isn't cheap.

Reputation: Tying public perception of your business to acts of kindness, social causes, and charity donations is great exposure. A positive reputation leads to customer and employee loyalty and drives customers to you instead of your competition.

Employee/team motivation: A positive work environment and ample compensation result in a productive workplace and enhanced loyalty. Appreciated team members work hard.

Collaborations: Businesses that share philosophies or social influencers can establish mutually beneficial relationships that result in shared customer bases and marketing budgets, new markets, and increased visibility.

Social Entrepreneurship

A social entrepreneur builds a business or organization to solve a societal problem. I think of them as entrepreneurs whose guiding principle is generosity. They are hungry in an entirely different way from the rest of the business world. Rather than professionally looking inward, developing skills, stepping up the ladder, and growing income, social entrepreneurs place community first.

The Acumen fellowship opened my eyes to social entrepreneurship. These specialty endeavours are more common in developing nations, where they create the greatest impact, but they're found in nearly every community worldwide. Where there is a desire to help others, there is usually someone behind it with business savvy to make it work.

Corporations have traditionally put programs in place to help communities in one way or another. They write cheques, and that's noble and more than worthy of the marketing attention it draws, but it falls on the reactive side of a societal issue. Social entrepreneurs are the disruptors of societal problems. Where there is disruption, there is innovation. This is a much more proactive mindset.

Social entrepreneurship is highly effective in developing nations because those governments often lack the infrastructure, knowledge, and desire to solve systemic problems that result from corrupt agendas. Citizens must look out for each other because their government won't. These entrepreneurs are in the streets, alongside the issues, and are better equipped to assess the problem and innovate ways to solve it.

Acumen participants manage free schools in Karachi for children whose parents cannot afford school fees. These social entrepreneurs have also created alliances with global banks to grant women in oppressed regions low-cost loans to start businesses, run ambulance services in areas with broken medical infrastructure, and innovate solar energy solutions in places with no electricity so that agriculture can be successful.

As mentioned previously, a fellow Acumen entrepreneur opened a mental health organization in Pakistan that assists with crisis intervention, connects those struggling with the help they need, and raises awareness that breaks through the cultural stigma of mental health issues. He's a Fulbright scholar from the University of Washington in Seattle, and he trained at top-notch universities to become a doctor. With his background, he could go anywhere and be successful; yet he combines his entrepreneurial drive with his passion for mental health support in his community.

These generous spirits take fewer benefits, less salary by half, and earn far less prestige, all to improve our world. I wanted to learn more so I could do better. I asked social entrepreneurs: What drives an entrepreneur toward the social end of business? I needed to know if I had that intangible within me.

Some answered that being a social entrepreneur is part of their role as humans. Some tied their generosity to a deep faith. Most were saddened that their fellow citizens were missing out on basic human pursuits—ones we all share—because of politics and greed. They inspired me with their courage to fight corruption, their selfless acts of sacrifice, and their prevailing messages of hope.

I joined the Acumen fellowship as AutoSahulat's founder. I left the program a changed businessman with an entrepreneurial heart. Acumen calmed me down so that I could see what I was doing in my life and illuminated what I *should* be doing. It reignited the sense of community I had left behind in Multan and never went back to retrieve. Some of my outreach was primarily self-serving, but a balance of promoting oneself and lifting others is the path to success that feels nice, resonates deeply, and leaves me with a renewed sense of purpose.

I began to open more doors for others. I nurtured relationships I could not post about, relationships that brought me no benefit, even as I extended a hand to others far down the road from me. I still volunteer and seek funding avenues for my fellow Acumen participants because that is a skill-set I can use to make an impact. Many of these individuals, their hearts overflowing with vision, are sharp in their industry. They can always use more business insight to bring everything together and ensure longevity. In these times, I leave my branding behind and quietly land in these spaces to lift others.

And it's amazing.

Life-affirming.

Usman was a contract employee on my sales team at Careem. Another department had hired him, but he was moved to mine before I joined the company. Usman was quiet—me-in-fifth-grade kind of quiet. We needed business volume, so I wanted Usman to go into the field to make cold calls with different companies.

We settled in for a chat over chai. Night café. You guessed it.

Initially, we sat alone. I recognized how he took an extraordinary interest in inanimate things—the leaving sun, the flow of activity near the ordering counter, the scrape of his thumbnail along the cup's lip. Once, I, too, found the quirks of behaviour that went unnoticed to be safe. I was certain glowing orbs and mythical creatures lived behind Usman's soulful gaze, which rarely met mine.

"I need someone to drop in these places, unsolicited, and make those connections," I said. "But if that's not something you want to do, I understand. I can look into other functions with the company that you may be more comfortable with."

He flashed a smile that didn't reach his eyes. "I want to learn."

"You'll be meeting new people. All day. Every day."

Usman nodded and rubbed his palms against the side seam of his jeans. He didn't speak, so I did.

I told him a half dozen stories of my worst cold calls. They were lean on the rudeness of others but generous in self-deprecation. Sales is an art, and few start out with the talent of Picasso. After he sobered from laughing, he opened up.

"I don't have your confidence."

"It will come."

"Will you help me? I want to learn this position."

He had let down his walls. In him was the light of ambition. Maybe that's what the glowing orbs were all along. Ambition. In him. In me. That was all I needed.

"Tomorrow, be at the office early. We'll go on sales calls together."

"Really?"

It was the most animated I'd seen Usman. I blamed the caffeine.

"You can observe me interacting with potential customers and see how I create a product story for them based on their input."

He nodded and took a bashful sip.

"Dress like you're me."

He looked down at his worn jeans, then splayed his arms to say, *I'm already there, sir.*

I laughed.

The next morning and every sunrise for the next month, Usman showed up dressed impeccably. Initially, he shadowed me. After three or four cold calls, I became his wingman. During downtime, I exposed him to software that managed our numbers and pipeline sheets that contained weekly reports. He stopped observing the flow of activity around him and found the confidence to match his inner light.

Today, Usman is a permanent employee who handles business-to-business analytics for all of Pakistan. He has onboarded numerous accounts and is integral to helping teams in other cities scale Careem for Business.

Before I left Careem, Usman was the first person I asked to shadow new hires. He'd take them out for chai, as animated as I'd ever seen him.

I no longer blamed the caffeine.

"I can't ask Talha," I said.

For the twentieth time, I skimmed the Antler announcement on my phone. The last paragraph made me nauseous. I tossed my cell on the café table and buried my face in my hands.

I had been selected for a two-month stint for a Global Founders program, but I did not have the resources to get there.

"What about your da—?"

"*No.*" Immediately, I wanted to bite back the harsh word. Imran bahi was only trying to help. But he knew enough to know that I'd rather do an army crawl through a pit of Pakistani black cobras than ask Father for money. With money came opinions. Muhammad Iqbal never had a shortage of opinions.

"Don't they have scholarships for this sort of thing?"

Imran bahi mowed through his almond cake, oblivious to the condition of my stomach. He was a friend but also Talha's cousin. Imran bahi was also one of my true supporters. Back when I joined the telecom Telenor and had to move, he had offered me a place in his home. I crashed there for six months. I couldn't continue to come to Talha with my hands clasped.

"No."

"Did you know you had to pay for airfare to Singapore?"

"I didn't think I'd win." I hated how that comment sounded even in my ears. Like the ten-year-old kid in the back of the classroom. "Thought I'd figure it out if the time came."

"That time is now, my friend." Imran bahi shoved my phone back at me with his sticky, honey-coated fingers. "Dial."

I sighed. At that point, anything to distract me from Imran bahi's chewing.

Talha picked up on the second ring. We made meaningless small talk. To detour the conversation away from his cousin's teasing comments, Imran bahi loudly launched into a setup I couldn't back down from.

"Gullu has a favour to ask you," Imran bahi said.

I made a face across the table. At that point, I wasn't sure I wanted to ask for help.

"Anything, man." Talha had always been open, empathetic, unwavering. Financial assistance, guidance in overcoming obstacles, mentoring—the guy was forever ready to lend a hand or an ear. He was my go-to when I faced such challenges.

I reminded him about the Antler program. He had been one of my biggest supporters in applying for it. He nearly lost his mind when I told him I was in.

Imran bahi grinned and nodded as if to say, *Now, strike now.*

I interrupted Talha's celebratory chatter. "See, there's a problem . . ."

He sobered on the line. "Yeah? What's up?"

"I have to find a way to Singapore. Everything else is covered."

A heartbeat passed. At most, two. "Say no more, brother," Talha said. "I'll have it to you within the hour."

I opened my mouth to talk him out of it. This was a huge ask—bigger than anything I'd asked before. But Antler was also bigger than anything that had happened to me before. My pride waged a mighty internal battle with my heart. *Say no more, brother*, and I was already boarding the aircraft in my imagination—but I didn't feel worthy of such generosity.

"I'll pay you back," I said.

"Yeah, you will. Remember us when you're some CEO at a big tech firm."

"You'll be part of my life story."

"I'd better be." Talha laughed.

We disconnected. Imran bahi and I remained at the café. A ravenous appetite returned. I felt like having a proper celebration.

Thirty minutes later, my cell chimed a notification. A much-needed sum had landed in my bank account.

I wanted my upcoming months and years to be generous. I wanted to find ways to give back—not just to Talha but also to so many others who lifted me when I needed it most. I didn't know what form that generosity would take, but I knew giving my all in Singapore was the surest path to that future.

10

BRING PEOPLE TO THE COURTYARD

Singapore's Buddha Tooth Relic Temple exhibits the kind of directness I crave. Buddha's left canine tooth is on display there. The shrine is five stories of peak Tang Dynasty architecture: timber walls framed in deep reds with golden studs; symmetry that makes you feel like the world is balanced; slanted bamboo rooflines that pitch steeply. Tones, both fiery and patterned, warmed the interior walls. Statues of everything from dragons to Buddhas outnumber human visitors. Bells chime, soft chants flow, incense burns, and flowers bloom in the rooftop garden. They might have named the temple Serenity or Sacred Light or Shi Fa Zhao after the abbot who conceptualized the place of worship, but they went with Buddha's left canine. As if to say that even a fragment of something special makes a difference in people's lives.

The Tooth Relic Temple is one of my favourite places, but not for the grandeur of its prayer halls or the welcoming aura of peace that shelters you like a Bedouin tent. On my first visit, I exited the temple and saw a Muslim mosque. Beside the mosque was a Hindu temple. A stone's throw away was a Methodist church. Visitors flowed and traded spaces and exchanged pleasantries. Their beliefs mattered; their differences did not.

This harmony is not possible in Pakistan.

Jews fled ages ago. There aren't many Christians. Hindus congregate in Pakistan's southern provinces. But even in predominantly Muslim areas, there is a breakdown into sects. Shi'ites have different mosques from Sunnis. People hold steadfast to their chosen path to enlightenment, often without questioning alternative perspectives. How are they so sure? They're born into it. They never question it, as if the divine wielded a map and a Sharpie and drew borders around spiritual destiny.

I did not want my children, who were nine and eight years old then, to grow up inside this echo chamber of fighting amongst the righteous. Nowhere in Pakistan could I show them that all humans have a right to uniqueness and that the order of the day is to accept differences and come together as one. That liberty, that freedom, that communication is nearly impossible to find in Pakistan. So, the first opportunity I got, I brought my kids to the Tooth Relic Temple.

We walked into the temple courtyard. "Look," I said, gesturing to the people streaming by. "Everyone lives happily. Nobody questions if you're right or wrong. No one is pointing fingers or judging. If you are Buddhist, great. If you are Muslim, great. If you are Christian, great. All individuals find meaning and fulfillment through various paths of spirituality. Respect the beliefs of others. Question. Be open to new experiences."

Their future will be better for this experience. Those who don't engage with the world beyond what they see every day become right-fighters. The internet brings to light those differences. How we frame those encounters is up to us.

Why Diversity Matters

More often than not, Pakistanis' minds are as closed as the nation's borders.

Our history has been sanitized so that we are the heroes of our own stories. Many buy into the false narratives about why the country cannot compete globally because the truth runs contrary to the reality they've crafted—that the infrastructure needs work, and that the world just won't give us a fair shake.

But truths hide below these surface arguments. Pakistan is not always a safe place to travel; therefore, people from diverse backgrounds rarely visit. Without an influx of diversity, cut off from the outside world, Pakistanis are born, live, and die by the same weak systems that have led to generational failure. Many of the country's political and establishment leaders hold dual citizenships with other nations. Corruption is rampant inside Pakistan because those who make and benefit from the crooked policies have backup plans outside the nation—an out for when things go south. Citizens want out, too, especially upper and middle-class people who are educated and have been exposed enough to developed countries to know that diversity brings opportunity for all.

Many citizens have lost hope.

Slowly, Pakistanis are starting to awaken to a different version of events than what we were told. They are beginning to question why we are at odds with India when we are culturally similar peoples. When I am traveling abroad, Indians are some of the first people I gravitate towards. We communicate, we connect, we become friends. But Pakistan cannot trade directly with India. Goods must travel through Dubai. Dubai comes out like an economic chieftain, and Pakistan is left stirring a pot of hostility toward India. Instead of perpetuating a silo mindset, leaders of the two countries should come to the table to create a cohesive strategy for the development of the entire region.

Contrast Pakistan's situation with the rise of India in the global marketplace. In the 1990s, Pakistan was more progressive in business than its eastern neighbour. India welcomed diversity but did not have a backup plan for its citizens. Indians cannot hold dual citizenship. Its people are all in or all out, which fosters an environment where talented people who contribute to their nation stay, and those who don't, leave. Also, India's politics did not impact its citizens' passport index ranking the way that the tragedy of 9/11 and the ensuing US War in Afghanistan affected Pakistanis' global mobility. India moved out of the developing-nation phase and built global influence—especially in the tech realm. Now, some of the most influential senior leadership roles in multinational companies are held by Indians. This puts them in solid positions to continue to grow their country's global influence.

Meanwhile, national companies stuck inside the borders of developing nations often receive taxpayer money and some kind of government funding. Therefore, when you look at their profits, they aren't very impressive. For national companies that perform well, regulations likely work in their favour. Private companies struggle, and their profits are tiny when compared to those of global giants. Overall, at national companies the sameness of experiences and skill sets stifles growth and minimizes exposure. Intellectual exchanges and candid discussions rarely occur.

Diversity brings out the best in a nation's people. Open borders and safe travel bring people with different ideas together. Shops and businesses open and thrive. Then multinational corporations see opportunity—a secure environment to embrace local talent and build a talented workforce that brings the best to the global community.

How Diversity Helps Businesses Thrive

A famous US-based Pakistani venture capitalist once commented that our biggest advantage and our biggest *dis*advantage is being Pakistani. In almost all respects, she was an outsider. And yet, growing up in a fringe, less-developed, unstable-adjacent nation conditions its people to resourcefulness and resilience. Jobs are not critical; they have never defined us; this is because we are always looking out for that next thing. This freedom from tunnel vision opens us to alternative paths and experiments. Our innovations are born out of tremendous need, not simply to improve on existing luxuries. Our hustle game is strong, and our drive is unparalleled.

We are programmed to believe that if we don't study, we won't survive. The broken die. Sounds extreme, right? People who push past borders of opportunity deliver more.

The same holds true of outsiders who have broken through other barriers of marginalization.

Your perspective is fresh, a game-changer for a team or a start-up. Here are some ways your employer benefits when they employ those of you who are from a diverse background.

> *Enhanced talent pool:* Your employment shows other prospective employees from diverse backgrounds a climate of inclusion. A wider talent pool attracts the most skillful in the field, which allows businesses to rise above their competition.
>
> *Compliance litmus test:* Your borders spotlight issues such as equal opportunity laws, fairness, equality, and social responsibility. Employing you forces businesses to hold themselves accountable and to move through daily operations holding to high ethical standards.
>
> *Wide-angle lens:* It's easy for businesses to fall into the trap of myopic vision—seeing only what's before them and the way operations have always been done. But typical scenarios and markets limit the long game in business. Your barriers act as corrective lenses that help businesses see farther and a broader picture.
>
> *Brand bounce:* Diversity is positive PR for any company. As an employee, you are proof that reaching past barriers isn't some marketing gimmick but organic to the company's ideology and brand.

Bringing new customers to the courtyard: Your unique background and experiences ensure that products and services appeal to a broader customer base—essentially, you. That's a bigger slice of the market and loyalty from customers who feel seen and heard.

Symbiosis: Diversity attracts diversity. Ideas and resources shared among partnerships, organizations, networks, and companies can turn seemingly impossible ideas into reality.

Barriers that make you feel like an outsider are an asset to any business. With a shift in mindset, disadvantages become superpowers. Groupthink and bias are harmful weak spots to start-ups and corporations alike. Diverse employees with challenging histories are uniquely calibrated to be watchful of potential pitfalls. Businesses thrive when these talents align with an ecosystem where employees feel valued and respected.

Your Role in Diversity

If you are in a corporate environment, you are not driving the diversity surrounding you. You may understand that diversity creates a vibrant business climate, but unless you find yourself on an interview team, your higher-ups are making the hiring decisions. However, employees can foster a diverse climate.

Educate. Share your culture with your team. Encourage them to do the same. Understanding is a great first step to diversity.

Mentor. Formally or informally, there is power in kindness and helping others.

Support sister projects. Suggest an outreach, charity, or organization across town or around the world that engagement with might bring mutual benefits for both entities.

Implement safe reporting. If your business does not already have a system for reporting harsh behaviour or discrimination, help it develop one that employees feel safe using.

Attend to outside-the-box areas. Diverse people have unique needs outside of work. Be cognizant that nonwork hours look different across your team. Come up with ideas and strategies so that all employees feel supported and can give their best during work hours.

Become a recruiter. Volunteer at your start-up or corporation to speak during recruitment events or to conduct pre-interviews. Seek ways to bring underrepresented communities to the employer's door.

One word of caution: Diversity initiatives include everyone. Resentment builds when some people's barriers are elevated over others'. Find ways to celebrate everyone on your team, even if you don't perceive their obstacles to be as formidable as yours. Remember, some barriers cannot be seen. Sometimes the most challenging ones are the ones inside that we share with no one.

9/11 and the War in Afghanistan in Brushstrokes

I was born in Pakistan but do not have the same mindset as the Pakistani leaders running the show.

Every human being is different. I don't deny that the world has bad players. Pakistan and other developing nations have their share. But those of us not involved in policymaking who are born into compromised regions are humans too. We have families. We have feelings, emotions, and career aspirations. We desire a future we can look forward to, same as anyone. So long as our background checks out, why should our birth nationality be problematic?

I've long believed that the problem stems from people's inability to separate individualism and nationalism.

During my time abroad on different work assignments, I've come to know the communities that comprise a rich and varied demographic. Though the energy between groups is mostly harmonious, sometimes there is a breakdown in trust. Small, ignorant factions sometimes perceive that nationals take all the gig and government jobs, while the minorities cross their borders, step over them, and snatch start-up and corporate positions. Then there are North Star aspirations. In the Southeast Asian start-up ecosystem, the North Star is Singapore. The depressing prevailing view is that others in the region are not doing enough to foster the kind of economic growth seen in Singapore in their own countries.

This mentality is not unique to Southeast Asia. How often have you groused about your nation's government and how it has failed to build a robust economy and grow opportunities?

People overlook what they already have.

I tell them, "Go to Pakistan. Look to developing nations and all they don't have. Then return with a new mindset. Cherish what you have, take it as a blessing, and elevate yourself. Beyond your borders, beyond your nation, you have value."

Individualism over nationalism.

A country's people are not its leaders. North Korea's leader, Kim Jung Un, is problematic. We cannot say the same about North Korea's people. They were simply born inside limiting borders.

True globalization cannot happen when the mindset isn't there yet.

Becoming That Diversity

Let's say your diversity interests stretch beyond merely welcoming those with barriers. If you want to actively participate in the diversity you wish to see by forging new and unprecedented routes, introspection will start you down the right path.

To lift yourself out of the restrictions that others place on you, you must first embrace your *I'm different* mindset. What sets you apart can become your superpower. Multinational corporations and start-ups will not recognize what you do not first see in yourself. Find a location and time when you can be thoughtful and answer the following questions:

1. How am I different from the employees around me? What part of my background sets me apart from others with similar skill-sets? What unique life experiences helped to shape the person I am? Your answers to these questions form the foundation of your story, which we explored in Chapter 2 on personal branding.

2. Finish this statement: If I had the courage and there were no limitations imposed on me, I would ______________________________

   ______________.

3. List three countries, corporations, or organizations that inspire you and most closely align with your identity. Ask yourself, *Where do I want to go?* Your answers can include moving past geography, but don't limit yourself to political borders. Tap into your philosophy, education, lifestyle, income, spirituality, family philosophy, or any other way you define success.

4. Based on your answers so far, short-list companies that intersect with your professional skill-set and, most importantly, align with your diversity-forward mindset.

5. Research people involved with your short-listed companies. Aim for the ones most active on social media and connect with them using the strategies outlined in Chapter 8 on networking. Give thoughtful comments on their posts. Aim to build a relationship. Even if you never become employed with the company, you will have extended a hand beyond the borders that have previously limited you. No network connection is ever wasted.

I did something similar to this exercise in 2016. Facebook was a company on my short list. In my mind, Facebook was a tech giant run by progressive-thinking people who were open to diversity and connected people to ideas in revolutionary ways. So, when an opportunity arose, a competition within Telenor, a telecommunications company, to outline how Facebook's Workplace platform benefited Telenor productivity, I jumped at the chance. I won the competition and joined three other winners from around the globe for a day at Facebook's Asian Pacific headquarters in Singapore.

Beyond the workplace ideas that seemed revolutionary at the time—open spaces to promote bonding and creativity, choosing projects you love, hack–build–make cycles of productivity, and employee equality, with no senior or junior hierarchy to interfere with progress—I was especially attuned to how my short-listed dream company scored high marks for embracing diversity. I needed to see myself there, thriving, despite my borders.

The cafeteria offerings catered to every nationality imaginable. The mantra *Be yourself at work* prioritized the celebration of all cultures and races. And the Extrinsic and Intrinsic resource teams were created with employees' well-being as a central priority. Touring Facebook Singapore quickly became one of my favourite business experiences, but not for the grandeur of the campus's 360-degree views, its trendy and vibrant furnishings, or the lightning speed of the move-fast-and-break-things mindset. A brief comment from an employee left a lasting impression.

"There's a temple in Chinatown. You have to go. It's amazing."

I visited the United Kingdom for three months to pursue my degree. Few things prepared me for the racism I encountered from British-born Pakistanis.

Sectarianism—the idea that one political or religious group inside a nation is better than another—is widespread in Pakistan. In part, this comes from an elitist mindset. Ties to the powerful equate to more opportunities, more favour, and more esteem.

In some ways, this is my reality.

A friend in Karachi once laid it out for me: "Your father was a high-ranking official. You're part of the 96 percent of Pakistanis who are Muslim. You're Sunni, and you are from Punjab." Suppose he'd had a crystal ball to gaze into my future. In that case, he'd have seen my role at Amazon Web Services, as head of Business Development Start-ups for six Southeast Asian countries, on planes every week, speaking to thousands of people and many venture capitalists, and said, "You see? This is what favour brings. Some of us are not so lucky." He believes those attributes—over which I had no control—are the main factors predicting a Pakistani's success.

He is not alone. Friction between the establishment and citizens is at an all-time high. Citizens blame the establishment for Pakistan's current struggles and the world's uneasy perception of our nation.

For this reason, in my professional career in Pakistan, I have rarely disclosed these attributes about myself unless required. I have four siblings. We are from the same family, sect, educational background, and hometown. We enjoyed the same perks because of Father's clout. Our family had a driver. And yet, my siblings' world remain limited.

This is how the world works, my family says.

No, this isn't how the world works, I insist.

You're stupid. What do you know?

They chose to stay. There is absolutely nothing wrong with their choice. Life is choices.

My belief in an individual's autonomy and how it is tied to destiny are alien. Unheard of in the dusty alleys of Multan.

I suspect the same thing happens in other developing nations. In all nations, really.

Individuals come up with all sorts of reasons to explain why one person achieves success and another does not. Rather than considering someone's hard work, merit, and life choices, they think about it through a lens of jealousy in a way that satisfies the narrative they have created in their mind. This prevents them from having to face things about themselves they'd rather not face.

Pakistani elitism is magnified overseas. During those three months in Britain, in the minds of UK-born Pakistanis, I was a *freshie*. Fresh from Pakistan. In their minds, I was culturally adjacent to them. We feasted on the same clay-oven flatbreads and *seekh-kabab*, skewered meat. We drove on the same side of the road. We felt an identical divide between our traditional parents' viewpoints and our more modern views that were shaped by growing up in a digital age. There were no barriers of language or customs between us. And yet, they fell into the trapped mindset that globalism isn't globalism unless it involves the United States or the United Kingdom, two countries we are heavily influenced by.

Because the British once ruled the Indian subcontinent—and America is, historically, an extension of Britain—British and US culture, everything from movies and music to philosophy and fashion, is idealized in Pakistan. If we communicate in English, we are taken seriously. If we communicate with a British or American accent, we're taken *extra* seriously. This embedded cultural lens of globalism is narrow and obsolete, yet still prevalent in Pakistan.

So, what could a dumb, socially inept boy from Multan, the kid everyone—including his family—had written off as a failure, understand about the greater world?

As it turned out, quite a bit.

11

KNOW YOUR EXITS

The Karakoram Highway, a 1,300 kilometre trek, is lined with crumbly, sand-coloured mountains and bright blue rivers that carve valleys into the terrain. Spectacular, if you're not snaking through the landscape during rainy season on the back of a rented 150cc Suzuki motorbike.

The solitariness of a bike ride is a prolonged meditation. Immersed in the rituals of the task, it's a profound and dangerous mental space. On one hand, it fosters a supreme level of reflection. Meaning-of-life kind of reflection. On the other hand, complacency climbs into the seat behind you and grabs hold of your waist. Defences downshift. My mind drifted to Saria, standing on a Lahore rooftop, fireworks splintering the sky. *What were you thinking? You always do this to us. Are you crazy?*

"Yes," I said to Nanga Parbat.

The snow-capped peak did not respond. Even the ninth-highest summit in the world had enough sense to step out of the rain.

Sibghat, our leader, rode ahead. He overtook a slow-moving truck with one taillight.

Mekael was next ahead of me. But he hung back.

I studied the hunched-over form of Mekael, a doctor friend from Islamabad. As exciting as the ten-hour road trip had seemed when he suggested it, the reality materialized as tedious and foolish.

I matched our speeds: sixty-four kilometres per hour.

Sibghat's bike lights were no longer visible through the morning cloud deck.

Damn.

We trailed the truck another half kilometre. Mekael's bike hugged the truck's back right bumper. His bike growled louder. At the straightaway, he positioned himself to overtake the vehicle, then thrust ahead.

The bike's back tire was the first to go. It slid horizontally in front of the truck's rear axle. His dark figure parted from the bike and collided with the asphalt.

My stomach bottomed out. My right hand and right foot braked. Hard. *Hard.*

Too hard.

The 150cc engine beneath me slipped away.

The four of us—Saria, the kids, and I—told no one in the family. Judgment about such things runs deep, and there would be questions I was not yet prepared to answer.

We were leaving Pakistan.

A logistics company packed the few belongings we wished to store and transported them to Multan ahead of us. My parents did not know the shipment was coming. Selecting items we wanted to keep was like playing out the housefire scenario: If you knew your family and pets would be safe, which few items would you grab? Saria approached the task with sentimentality. The kids didn't yet know the shift in perspective to come—that what they valued now may not be the same things they valued when they returned. That *they* might not be the same when they returned.

Me? I took clothes and magnets.

The magnets wreaked havoc with luggage scanners at the Karachi airport.

Fridge magnets are a tangible representation of the places I have travelled, and they don't take up much room. I can't say why I started the collection. Maybe they give me a sense of belonging to the greater community of world travellers. Maybe my identity is wrapped up in being the guy who never stayed in one place for long. Maybe the visceral response I get from seeing them when I grab my coffee creamer each morning is a jolt more potent than caffeine.

We sold everything else.

The day my Toyota Vigo and my red Benelli 250 bike drove away pinched a little. A tightness settled in my chest. Odd that it hadn't happened when I handed in my resignation to Careem but only when such big, material, freedom-embracing parts of my life rolled away.

Selling those items was the point of no return for me. But I was dreading the exit that I had prayed would come for so long. The four of us would be fine. I was safe in that conviction. But the collateral damage to those we left behind would endure. In Pakistan, you are born, educated, work, marry someone from a strong background, make a family, get a better house, and die. You have your roots, so you stay and deliver.

On the day the shipment was set for delivery, we took a flight from Karachi to Multan.

The city hadn't changed. My village hadn't changed. Even my breathing skipped ahead of the pace of life over 800 kilometres away from the city. Seconds crawled. Ten years in Multan is equal to five years in Lahore. Five years in Lahore is equivalent to three years in Karachi. Three years in Karachi is six months in the developed world. In Multan, people said close-minded things. I was ten years old all over again.

We gathered over a meal. Aromas of spicy meat, curry-and-tamarind vegetables, and fragrant rice wafted from the feast. My brother Mustansar brought his wife from the village. Nasir came, as supportive as ever. My sisters, Ghazala, and Nadia, were there. In my absence, they had grown into miniature versions of Mother, in beauty and in thought.

I waited until full digestion set in. My chest felt like a scuba tank—heavy, pressurized—with a forbidden bubble of trapped moisture waiting to surface. Dad was often cantankerous when hungry. Mom was prone to bombastic shouting displays and arms that moved like a *houbara bustard* with a wingspan to strike that was equally impressive. Besides, difficult truths are more easily digested when bellies are warm.

Absurd that I should have wanted to cushion the announcement of our future. We were excited. For us, they should be happy.

Just before Mom passed around the sweets, I took Saria's hand and said, "We have something to tell everyone."

Chewing stopped. A few sets of eyes lowered to Saria's midsection. Ridiculous that they might expect another bundle given the ages of our children.

"I got a job overseas. Malaysia. We're leaving Pakistan."

The words opened a pressure valve. The rest came out in a rush of air. I told them about my position with a big tech corporation, detailed some of my responsibilities, reminded them that it was a dream come true, and assured them of the top-notch schools and amazing opportunities for my family. They peppered me with questions that were upbeat and inquisitive. I squeezed Saria's hand. The release felt welcome until I looked at Mom's face.

She was not bombastic and did not strike with her wingspan. She did not stand to clear the dishes to preoccupy herself. She exhibited none of the behaviours that she had in the past when I'd mentioned moving abroad. Instead, she pinched off my breathing line with a one-word question.

"When?"

"Three days. After we drive to Lahore to say goodbye there."

Her expression did not indicate she heard me. I had never seen her so blank. Part of me witnessed the upturn of her mouth into the trace of a smile—at the least, a tightening of her lips because I am prone to such departures of positivity. The greatest portion of me recognized the judgment in her controlled nod.

Our belongings arrived then. While the kids regaled the family with all they had learned about Malaysia in their research, Dad and I went out to accept the shipment. Nestled beside boxes was a guitar-shaped case. I had let so much go, but not the guitar.

Father stood beside me and sighed. "Are you sure about this?"

"Can we ever really be sure about anything?"

He nodded. He looked older than I remembered. How much deeper would the lines in his expression grow with distance and time? Dad was never one for technology. We could barely get him on a video call. A sliver of doubt lodged in my throat. Muscles there tightened.

Pakistani men talk about successes, politics, women, and money—not necessarily in that order. Feelings were never up for discussion.

"Proud of you, *beta*."

Son.

A stinging gathered in my sinuses, behind my eyes. Pakistani men are not predisposed to crying. I made an exception that day.

Muhammad Iqbal came from rural places, pre-1947. Though he had no father, he became one. He was scolded into giving up his dream so that I could live. There was no way he would rip my opportunity to shreds.

Chances are, if you've called a customer service line, you've been forwarded to someone at a call centre in Pakistan. It's possible we spoke. Call centres are a huge industry in Pakistan because we learn English from a young age. The job isn't challenging, but it is tough. You put on your headset and brace yourself for an entire shift of mental adversity—three to four hundred people's worth.

If the call centre is international, most customers who call are from

Western countries. Some are nice. Most are not. You're the warm body on the other end of whatever problem they have, so they're already amped up before you've said hello. They ask you about packages, and sometimes they shout. If one rupee or dollar is in question, they want it deducted.

I worked at my first call centre for a few months. They assigned me the night shift. One of my friends worked there as well. The boss caught him smoking a joint. He was fired. Because I was his friend, I was also fired.

I hopped immediately to a local call centre. I had married Saria the previous year, and she was pregnant with Ibrahim when I joined. On the fifteen-minute breaks at the call centre, workers headed up to the entrance area to smoke cigarettes, make each other laugh in the name of sanity, and shout at and abuse the worst callers right back.

For seven months, I worked from four in the afternoon to midnight. When my family got up to start their day, I was usually sleeping. My connection with my family suffered. I lost myself in the vampirish hours. If you had asked me my goal at that time—my biggest measure of success—I would have said, *Transferring to a day shift.*

I tried, but it never happened. I was one warm body inside a massive system. Eventually, I resigned.

One involuntary exit. One voluntary exit.

Both were filled with lessons beyond *guilt by association* and *the real reason vampires are so cranky.*

Job exits mark significant transitions in life. They offer a chance to adapt to new technologies and reinvent ourselves if we don't like who we see in the mirror. Had I not walked away from the second call centre, I would not have redefined my definition of success. I was tired and had set a shamefully low bar.

The uncertainty of a job exit does not have to be a negative emotional experience. Resilience is a muscle that must be used to be strengthened. No matter what you call it—uncertainty or desperation—both states of being force you into embracing that next new thing. And, if you learn by force that you'll be fine on the other end, you're more willing to voluntarily exit from situations where you're stagnating—with another opportunity lined up ahead of time, of course.

Job exits also act as temporary reminders that life is more than work. Sure, we need money to survive, but those first hours and days after an exit are like staying home from school on a sick day. You awaken to nuances of life that moved forward while you focused your attention elsewhere.

I've had more jobs than I can count. Contract and salary. This is a common experience in developing nations. We work. We hustle to survive and provide for our families with little left over. We sleep. And then we do it again the next day. I have experienced bureaucratic misconduct from the inside out, had pay withheld for six-month stretches, and taken jobs solely because of family pressures and being a provider. I started slow and on a basic level. Along the way, I accumulated interests that solidified around ideas and philosophies that guided me down a path.

But the *path* has a troubling secret: it doesn't show you the end.

The path doesn't even really show you it's *the* path.

People envision their desired outcomes. They sample the path they believe will lead them where they want to go. But once they commit to the path, they find it diverges into countless other roads. Roads that demand choices. Sometimes those choices lead to outcomes no longer wanted.

There is no shame in turning around. Indeed, finding untrodden, unconventional trails between roads should be celebrated.

I never applied for my current role. I aimed to do sales for big tech, but that's not where I landed. I am grateful I turned around and set out in an alternate direction. I had already conquered sales. From those first few steps on my journey, I could not see that new dreams awaited me.

Exits

A fine line exists between adaptability and perseverance.

These are two sides of the same coin of change. One carries the promise of growth; the other may compromise your long-term well-being.

The first impulse to leave a job may be due to temporary factors. Every job has these moments. If the notion becomes more frequent or persists for long periods, it may be time to evaluate whether you have outgrown your position. Ask yourself the following questions to gain better insight:

1. *Are the plans I once had with this job still viable?*
2. *Does this role align with my long-term goals and career aspirations?*
3. *Am I moving forward?*
4. *What are the positive aspects of the challenges I'm facing?*
5. *Have I taken the time to cherish what I have now?*
6. *Are my supervisors aware that I am struggling? Have I sought mentorship in my current role?*
7. *Is growth encouraged? Can I use this position to learn new skills for the future?*
8. *Have I researched my industry to identify areas of growth and innovation?*
9. *Am I limiting myself with a narrow view of success?*
10. *Am I thinking objectively or emotionally? Proactively or reactively?*
11. *Have I turned my job failures into opportunities to learn?*

12. *Are the job challenges temporary or more indicative of a long-term trajectory?*
13. *Have I attempted different strategies to make the job palatable?*
14. *Does this job have a positive impact on my physical and mental health?*
15. *Are there trusted colleagues in whom I can confide?*
16. *What factors make the exit risky? Can I create a plan to mitigate those risk factors?*
17. *Is my branding and storytelling in place to seek out alternative options?*
18. *Have I continued to nurture and grow my network?*
19. *Have I innovated myself, independent of this job?*
20. *Am I willing to apply and interview for jobs in my industry that I never intend to accept?*
21. *Am I willing to consider adjacent opportunities that lead me in new directions?*
22. *What do I lose by exiting? What do I gain?*
23. *If the me twenty years from now returned to give me advice, what would that advice be?*

Seeking advice should be an important component in your exit considerations. Discretion and trust go without saying, but you should also consider populating your advisory board with a wider variety of people. Mentors in your industry who are not with your employer provide a valuable perspective. Career counsellors help you expand on the above questions and keep your career aims at the forefront of any decision.

Be watchful for signs. At critical points in my career that necessitated an exit, a sign almost always came in the weeks and months prior. A sign could be making a costly mistake or meeting someone by chance. Learn to listen to your intuition. That voice inside you picks up on signals you ignore while you're trying to make everything work.

Sometimes the greater danger lies in *not* exiting. Time is the ultimate chaos. Time passes, whether you're chasing your goals with fire or coasting. Live your professional life with intent.

Interviewing

Antler's founder, Magnus Grimeland, loves the word *grit*. To him, someone who displays *grit* is a motivated self-starter, has that one niche area of stratospheric expertise, and has the drive and integrity to lead people to all the right places. I still vividly remember his first talk to our founders' cohort in Singapore.

When I took on responsibilities requiring me to seek grit in others, I reflected on what that word meant to me. To me, grit is the intangible power to move people, ideas, and beliefs. I don't always know where to seek grit, but I know it when I find it.

Before interviews, I don't look at résumés. Résumés are cooked, perfected versions of your work history. I rarely glean anything from them. I don't want to see your academics; I want to see *you*. No doubt, this stems from decades of people misjudging me for not following conventional paths in business. I blazed trails where there were no paths or roads. I want to work with those who aren't afraid to do the same.

I first investigate the candidate on social media—primarily the sites that are professionally driven. Manufacturing a brand and sustaining it over a longer period is difficult. Cracks of insincerity tend to show. From this social media review, I learn about the candidate's current or most recent job. That's the only work history I want to know before the interview—the rest I want to learn through the candidate's story.

During an interview, I search for emotions. I want to catch people slightly off-guard. I will never ask overly googled questions like *Why do you want this job?* or *Why are you good for this role?* Passion and hunger can be faked in an interview, so anything that draws candidates left of centre gives me insight into their authentic self. I'm looking for footholds into personal brands. I want to hear stories—how they are *different*—in a way that compels me to want to know more. I listen for ways that the candidate's story will inform me, change my mind about something, or perhaps change me.

If I ask them to describe themselves, they probably have rehearsed answers. They will give me their version of the public mask that we all wear, which tells me nothing. But if I ask *How would your best friend describe you?* or *How would the last person who disagreed with you describe you?* I'm shifting their perspective. This is also my litmus test for honesty. I'd rather someone answer candidly than tell me something I want to hear; there's simply no room for that kind of pandering in the business environments I create. Down the road, I don't want to realize that I hired the wrong person because I fell for their facade.

Nerves create a barrier to getting to know candidates. An interview is a short window of time, but I try to create relationships to break down those barriers.

Once people open up in an interview, it's fairly easy to gauge what they want, what kind of heart they have. They may give answers about innovation and how they crave the risk inherent in start-ups, but if I learn they're the primary caregiver for their nana and create thirty-second viral videos in which she gives humorous advice about life, that candidate is going to be a different kind of wonderful than what their rehearsed words might have expressed.

I also want to know what applicants know about the company, not just the job opening of interest. Myopic vision—that short-sighted, narrow focus on one available position—turns me off from the strongest candidates. I don't want an island; I want a team. I want people who are natural extensions of all parts of a company, not just governors of their own desks.

Interviewers have vulnerable spots. Biases they fight against. Candidates who have similar backgrounds to me, the perpetual outsiders, and those who have failed and missed out on opportunities but who want a second chance to prove themselves are *my* bias. I don't worry so much about the graduates from prestigious universities. An applicant with stellar academics who comes to me professionally stable will get hired by that next great company. Candidates who craft a compelling story and inspire me to remember them after they're gone—even if they're memorable for something unrelated to the position or business—are my professional catnip. I want to open doors for them that may have been shut.

It worked for me.

Preparing for an interview with me is different. Then again, what about me and my story *isn't* different? Some other things to remember beyond the conventional advice:

> *Before your interview, get to know the interviewers.* Go through their social media profiles. Watch professional content videos your interviewers have recorded. Read through posts and articles to find out what preoccupies their minds. They're doing the same for you, so why not flip the script? Reflect on their brands and their stories to find nodes of connection to yours. Make notes of those things that may authentically unify you during the interview.
>
> *Know your brand and your story.* Everyone has a story to tell. Learn how to tell a great one. Test it on new people you meet at parties or networking events and shape it accordingly. Note the parts of your story that people consistently respond to. Those beats in your story are the places of universal connection.
>
> *Do your homework.* Find out where the company stands in the bigger ecosystem. Know how the company is performing against the competition, the company's dream for the

future, and what the company values most. Reflect on your research. Be able to articulate the ways your enlightened top-down view of the company aligns with you.

"We should go back," I said. "Plan for a time when the weather is better."

We had paused our near-death motorcycle trek. The plan was to discuss next steps over *chai* and dislodge our hearts from our throats.

Sibghat, our leader and my colleague from Careem, erupted like I'd suggested we join a circus troupe and bike across the river on a high wire. "It's the first day! I knew we shouldn't have brought you! You're too green."

"We've been on the road since four a.m." My tone channelled twelve hours of lower-back pain and swallowed bugs. "I can't see through the drizzle without my shield, and I can't see the road clearly *through* my shield."

"What will turning back solve?" Sibghat fired off. "You're driving through the same rain."

Weeks before, he'd taught me how to ride. His patience was infinite in basic accelerator and brake knowledge. Apparently, the limit to his tolerance was found in fear.

"We're closer to home than we are to Hunza."

Mekael wandered between us in a vague, exhausted sort of way. Salt-and-pepper hair that had been helmet protected nested on his head like the starter wool for a brush fire, uselessly soaked. He glanced around at the outbuildings. The structure was a rest stop with food and water fountains for drinking and washing. In the dim, drizzly light, the place was the stuff of Abde's horror tales.

"Let's just stay here awhile," Mekael said.

At that point, I would have surrendered my right kidney to the black market for a carpet or a dirty cloth to lay on, so long as it was out of the rain. Every inch of my gear looked like I'd plunged it into the Hunza River.

Three people had cautioned me against taking this trip, citing safety concerns. Not all the concerns related to keeping cars on the treacherous road.

"We're almost to our next stop," Sibghat said. "A few kilometres, tops."

I looked at the doctor.

He nodded.

Mental note: *Mekael does not get my kidney.*

We half-heartedly and cautiously drove ahead to the predetermined stop along the Islamabad–Hunza route. Mekael was eerily quiet. For a physician accustomed to dealing with death, he missed the signs of shock in himself.

For the most part, our gear had protected us. We sipped chai in bristling silence until Mekael found his words.

"Let's go home."

The man knew his exit.

I thought none of us had the guts to argue, especially with the guy whose neck had been centimetres from a truck's tread clawing the road, until Sibghat spoke.

"We should ride a little farther. Then decide."

A cursory check of the bikes wasn't the same as a full inspection. I didn't have the energy to fight him.

We altered our itinerary to include an unplanned overnight stay, spending the night there before continuing with our original travel plan. The compromise proved helpful to morale. We stopped at Babusar Top, one of the most dangerous mountain passes in the world, where brake failure is the most common cause of death. The view was unparalleled. It wasn't me pushing this time, but I'm glad we listened to Sibghat and kept going. Mekael regained his confidence on the bike, so we pressed on with our journey. Taking us to Hunza and Attabad Lake and back, the trip unfolded as planned and will always be cherished by me.

I also needed the reminder that Saria was right: I am crazy.

12

INSIDE OUT

At the edge of Singapore's Marina Bay, a seventy-ton concrete statue, half mermaid and half lion, spews a firehose-calibre projectile of water into the inlet. Fish scales are said to represent the city's modest beginnings as a fishing village; the lion comes from the city's original name, *Singapura*, which means *Lion City* in Malay.

My name, Ghazanfar, has Arabic roots and translates to "Lion." Whether this is a coincidence or not, I'm unsure.

I'm standing alone on a nearby jetty. Fireworks have just ended—Singapore's Independence celebration that August 9th. The night was electric, and filled with weary parents, children up past bedtime, lovers lingering so they didn't have to say goodnight, and the carefree shouts of the youth who had it in them to party all night.

Orbs glowed.

A mythical creature, larger than any I could imagine, loomed over me.

But this was no *Roshan-e-Pul* moment. Here, in Singapore, I had wanted to mix, to fit in. Hadn't I coveted this Antler opportunity more than every next breath? Hadn't I sacrificed nearly everything to be here?

And yet . . .

To inhale deeply brought me in touch with the sensation of hollowness in my legs and the iron bars of my ribs. My mind drifted, detached from the tangible displays of joy surrounding me, the surest derealization I'd ever known. It all felt like a mistake.

I considered what a seventy-ton depiction of my two halves would be. On one hand, I identified with elephants. Elephants were prone to displacement, migratory in nature, and—at over six feet tall—they tower over most other creatures around them. For the other half, I racked my brain to come up with a compatible creature of prowess and distinction. All I could summon was an ant: disciplined, frugal. A diligent worker. The combination would be impossible to depict as a statue—half elephant, half ant—yet the imagined attempt lightened my mood.

Antler had given each founder participating in the program five thousand Singaporean dollars per month to pay for accommodations; it was enough to secure nice rooms or a condo, even in such an expensive city. I opted to stay at hostels. Shared bathrooms and bunk beds were small inconveniences to offset the money I saved for my start-up. I sent the remainder home to help the family.

When hostels were overbooked, I reverted to a tactic I'd used earlier in life and spent the night at one of those flexible-office-space places that were open all night. With no air-conditioning past work hours and sensor lights that made the floor glow like a grid of laser tripwires, sleep was fleeting at best. In the morning, I'd wash up in the restroom and step into a crisp ensemble of brightness and energy.

Most days, I stared at my reflection and questioned why I was making such sacrifices—sleeping on floors and cots, going hungry to save money, losing touch with Saria, missing my children's evolution into pint-sized humans over weeks that I could not retrieve. I doubted everything.

I suspect others who push past borders doubt everything too.

The journey past limitations never truly ends. Even when external borders crumble, the internal ones persist. Beyond the topics we've discussed already—willingness to embrace failure, taking steps beyond what is comfortable, gathering new skills, and flexing resilience like a muscle—the Antler experience was the ultimate challenge to my limiting beliefs. I had to *know*—to the depths of my lion heart—that I was no longer that kid in the back of the classroom, the call-centre worker, the boy who believed the things his father said about him, the man who would be forever defined by his restrictive geography. I was an elephant, an ant, and a founder.

Pushing past your borders requires courage. Sometimes you will find yourself on the floor unable to sleep or on a jetty wondering when you gave yourself permission to sacrifice so much more than you intended. In those moments, congratulate yourself for stretching your belief system.

What is behind you is safe.

What lies ahead is where you're meant to be.

Saria will tell you I push.

I do.

Now comes the time for me to push you. Imagine we're together on that rooftop in Lahore, nothing but broken furniture, incinerated plants, and forbidden drinks around. Or at one of my favourite outdoor cafés in Karachi, sipping chai in the leaving sun.

Pakistan is beautiful, even when it isn't.

As an outsider in business, you want truths. Unpopular truths. Truths that others in business are too afraid to say, but truths that will finally lift you out of obscurity and give you a shot at being a business insider. By now, you know me. You've taken this trip with me. I've literally sold shit in one of the most opportunity-averse and inhospitable places on the planet. If I can summit global big tech, anything for you is possible. But we must speak in truths.

If you want to grow professionally, if you're looking into the business ecosystem from the outside and want to be on the inside, you must be part of something innovative. Position yourself at the forefront of creation. Right now, that explosive threshold is technology. Artificial intelligence is set to disrupt every industry, so why wouldn't you avail yourself and level up by using it? In a few years, the next best thing may be elsewhere. Follow where innovation goes and get on its leading edge.

Don't get into a start-up if you don't have the stomach for it. Risk-averse people need not apply. There's nothing wrong with safe corporate jobs while you have outside responsibilities. There's nothing wrong with corporate jobs, period. Some people do not hunger to grow, and that's okay. Just don't bemoan your lack of opportunities and salary down the line if you choose the safe path.

Find passion in *something* you're doing each day. Even if the seed or core idea of a job or project doesn't ignite you, some aspect of it will allow you to grow and find opportunities. Passions are fickle. They play out and extinguish. At one time, my passion was to be a rock star. Then I wanted to go to Mars. Passions are largely based on circumstance—what is happening externally and internally. Follow your interests until new paths become clear.

Make sacrifices. If you don't sacrifice, you will not grow rapidly. Don't shy away if your supervisor asks you to do something extra. If a customer needs you on the weekend, find the time. If you don't make those sacrifices, someone else will. With the wrong attitude, you *will* get left behind.

If you're not failing, you're not trying. Periodic failure means you're trying *something*. Good for you. Challenge the status quo. Head in a direction, even if your path is wayward and you must backtrack. If you want to change your life, your approach must be radical. If failure becomes a habit, it's time to look closer and change your tactics.

Make personal branding, storytelling, and networking part of your daily routine. Do not wait for storms. No one will listen on your timetable.

If you're serious about a job, don't send people your résumé via social media and ask them to hire you. They won't look at it. They shouldn't. Use job sites and formal application channels to investigate and gather information to get yourself short-listed. Consider why you're a good fit for the opportunity. Deepen your interview preparations. These steps show a level of seriousness you'll need to approach your network.

Plan the time to innovate yourself. If you don't prioritize it, it won't happen. I add training to my weekends because I'm too distracted by my everyday roles and responsibilities during the workweek to give new skills the added focus they deserve. Prioritize your commitment to yourself, and your growth will be exponential.

Strike a balance when showcasing your employer in developing your personal brand. Including the company name in your social media headlines or bio can be beneficial at times, especially with a compelling reason. While your journey indeed transcends any single job experience or company, strategically associating yourself with a notable employer or success can sometimes enhance your professional image. Demonstrating a mindful connection to a company's success, while also highlighting your individual contributions and growth, shows potential employers your capacity for impact within organizational success.

Don't pay for premium access on social media sites. It's expensive and doesn't give you much advantage. Most of us can search and message anyone anytime. Unless you have a strong product to sell or a personal brand or clout that compels people to respond to your message, you're wasting money on a subscription. Use that money to develop yourself. Become a thoughtful responder to your targets' content. Have fruitful and authentic exchanges on their posts. Be remembered for the right things.

Social media platforms that offer you the ability to post thirty or sixty second video reels are a great place to invite opportunities. Reels give you two possible advantages. First, video is a brisk and engaging way to tell your story and advance your brand. Second, people who consistently release reels sometimes earn money from the platform. You may find that creating and putting out content supersedes your original intent, that it's the opportunity you were originally pursuing. This happened to an acquaintance of mine in Pakistan. After he reached a hundred thousand followers, companies approached him with job offers. He sustained and thrived on the platform as an influencer until the perfect offer came along.

The most difficult of all truths is that you will have to work harder, be more, and do more because of what makes you an outsider. But this reality is two sides of the same coin. Wallow in bitterness or use adversity as a catalyst to become the best version of yourself.

My relationship with the word *home* is complex.

Sometimes, the idea of home is rigid—a fixed line cluttered with way stations: Dad's military background and moving from one city to another, from Karachi to Rawalpindi, and traveling nearly every provincial road in between, moving from Europe to Southeast Asia. But way stations are not home. They are stopping points on a line of travel.

Most times, the idea of home is fluid—the ever-changing geographical and intellectual spaces where I am accepted. Home is a diverse place, free of borders, where people are defined by personal choice, not the poor decisions of others.

Home is Saria and my children.

Business exists on a continuum. Success drives us to move along that continuum, to re-evaluate as we grow, and to want new and different things. I want to go home and open a place for people to be near the ocean, to enjoy the Arabian Sea at sunset, pink and glossy and merciful, without fearing for their safety. I want to become the change I wish to see for Pakistan, something that cannot be done while inhabiting big tech, a unicorn, or a multinational corporation. I want to run a 100 million dollar venture capitalist firm—I've experienced all roles in the start-up ecosystem except that one.

Because of my varied experience, my network lives in all these spaces. It's about relationships. At any one time, I could make these things happen.

Whatever I decide, it will be a disruption.

Whatever you decide, make it a disruption. For the world. For your corner of the world.

That is how we innovate.

I came from nothing, felt like nothing, and was nothing—a complete outsider in every sense.

And yet . . .

ABOUT THE AUTHOR

Ghazanfar Iqbal stands at the forefront of business development in the dynamic startup ecosystems of several Asian markets as the Head of Business Development Startups at Amazon Web Services (AWS). His journey, spanning over a decade, is marked by diverse roles and accomplishments, including entrepreneurship, sales, marketing, and cloud computing.

Ghazanfar's passion lies in nurturing the growth of startups across Asia, from emerging to mature markets, playing a key role in AWS's expansion and in uence. In his book, Ghazanfar takes a deep dive into his personal and professional journey, highlighting his persistence, travel experiences, and the invaluable lessons learned from failures.

His past roles include serving as the Country Head of Sales at Careem and co-founding the rst Pakistani startup AutoSahulat funded by Antler, a global venture capital and accelerator organization. An Acumen Fellow, Ghazanfar's story is a testament to resilience, innovation, and the power of dreaming big.

Find him on LinkedIn:
https://www.linkedin.com/in/ghazanfar-iqbal/